SEXUAL CHALLENGES

Navigating Your Course Through Troubled Waters to Loving Relationships

To Jean,
  Dear friend and
fellow group member —
        Love,
         Gene

July 27, 1996

SEXUAL CHALLENGES

Navigating Your Course Through Troubled Waters to Loving Relationships

by

Barbara Childers, M.S.W., Ph.D. & Eugenie G. Wheeler, M.S.W., L.C.S.W.

Pathfinder Publishing

Ventura, California

SEXUAL CHALLENGES

Published by:
Pathfinder Publishing of California
458 Dorothy Avenue
Ventura, CA 93003
(805) 642-9278

Library of Congress Cataloging-in-Publication Data

Childers, Barbara, 1938-
    Sexual challenges : navigating your course through troubled waters to loving relationships / by Barbara Childers & Eugenie G. Wheeler.
        p.   cm.
    Includes index.
    ISBN No. 0-934793-58-1
    1. Sex instruction. 2. Hygiene, Sexual, 3. Love. 4. Man-woman relationships. I. Wheeler, Eugenie G., 1918- . II. Title.
HQ56.C552   1996
613.9'07--dc20   96-7507
                                                    CIP

DEDICATION

To our husbands in appreciation for their support, devotion, and inspiration.

FOREWORD

To successfully meet the challenges to intimacy and interpersonal satisfaction, one cannot simply learn the homilies of the past. We now know that the low divorce rates in grandma's and grandpa's generation were not related to satisfying marital relationships, but more to cultural norms, sanctions, and constraints. Many more of our grandmothers would have left their marriage nests if there had been greater employment opportunities for them and if religious and family proscriptions were not so severe.

Nor will a desperate search for "happiness" uncover that treasured relationship — where all of one's needs are met by that "perfect" partner. In their incisive and extraordinarily clearly written book, Barbara Childers and Eugenie Wheeler cast the spotlight on those day-to-day realities, responsibilities, and reciprocities that can help people achieve satisfaction in relationships. In providing many sound suggestions and intuitive recommendations, Childers and Wheeler avoid the pitfall of viewing sex as a goal in its own right. This is no "sex therapy manual," but a comprehensive approach to the "why" and "how" of commitment and companionship, prerequisites to safe and satisfying sex.

The authors emphasize the importance of communication skills — both accurate social perception, empathy, and verbal and nonverbal expressiveness — in developing and sustaining social and physical intimacy and pleasure. This is a book that should be read by the teenager just starting to explore relationships, young and mature adults, and seniors — the messages that fill every page are equally relevant to all age groups. And the overall message is of hope and positive outcomes that can be achieved when sexual challenges are met on the field of established relationships filled with affection, concern and respect. These challenges have been met and won by Barbara Childers and Eugenie Wheeler in their longstanding marriages and they can be met by you.

Robert Paul Liberman, M.D.
Professor of Psychiatry
UCLA School of Medicine
Author of *Handbook of Marital Therapy*

TABLE OF CONTENTS

INTRODUCTION

This book is a guide to safe, satisfying, sexual, loving, relationships in a time of changing and confusing sexual roles. It's about achieving a healthy sex life when the fear and reality of sexually transmitted diseases, some incurable, are rampant. We live in an age when the sexual expectations of both men and women are in a stage of transition. Some men are exhilarated while others are disconcerted when women are more direct and sexually demanding. Some women delight in a partner that shares home and work responsibilities, while others prefer to stay in more traditional roles. Our goal is to help you identify and follow your own needs and values. This book is a compass to keep you from floundering among the multiple and often contradictory sexual messages that bombard you from the media, parents, religions, and individuals.

The authors have counseled with hundreds of men and women who wanted to find satisfactory ways of responding to these and similar sexual challenges. We wrote this book for adults of all ages: for young people, who are discovering their sexuality; for the middle-aged, some of whom may be back in the world of dating, seeking new partners and starting new lives after being divorced or widowed;

and for older people, who may find it difficult to acknowledge that they still have sexual feelings or the need for intimate companionship. You may find it unusual that we are "lumping" together young adults, middle-aged, and seniors, but we believe that the principles governing good sexual relationships apply at every age, even though the application of them may take different forms at various stages in life. The more we study sexual solutions to sexual challenges, the more we think the differences are related to personality and philosophy rather than to age. For example, some conservative fundamentalist folks in their early twenties still view the husband's role as rightfully authoritarian. At the same time the feminist movement has had an impact on some elderly couples who started out with traditional values and now enjoy working towards a more equal partnership. Sexual relationships are so personal, so individual, that generalizations can be misleading. The term "partner" is used rather than "husband," "wife" or "spouse" so no group or indvidual will feel excluded. Using case examples and vignettes makes it easier to identify with the situations and extract the information that can be of the most value to you.

Statistics are not only hard to come by, but often misleading. We interviewed a wide range of men and women; from celibate young adults to promiscuous older ones, and found alcoholism and other forms of substance abuse crossing generational, and just about every other kind of line. We hope all adults, whether married or single, male or female, in their twenties, fifties or eighties, lesbian or gay, in good health or physically challenged, will find some insights, helpful guidelines, and support, in the following pages.

You start this journey by clarifying your course and setting goals for loving relationships. What will happiness look like for you once you have achieved it? Described are some typical storms, and hazards that can take you off course. You may want to add some of your own. You will develop your sexual self-contract as you read through the book. This will serve as a foundation for establishing your own personal chart for your sexual well being and will facilitate your reaching your goals.

Myths are distinguished from reality, and fiction from fact in the sexual maze. Then you will focus on who you are as a sexual being, and the many influences that have contributed to where you are now.

Once your direction and plans are firm, developing effective sexual communication skills lead toward a careful examination of how to take good care of yourself, both emotionally and physically.

When your best efforts are not enough, and you have been damaged, ways to expedite your healing and rehabilitation are addressed. The end of the book helps you to integrate the skills and knowledge gained through the use of your sexual self contract that you have been developing as you read through each chapter. At the end of the book you are encouraged to find a healthy balance, and to affirm your sexual self and establish the high quality, loving relationship that is your goal.

We, the authors, have had years of experience in couple counseling, including marital therapy. We've experimented with many approaches (both having taught various approaches to psychotherapy) including behavior modification, assertive training, reality therapy, anxiety management training, etc.

This book is a melange of the approaches we think work best. You can apply them with or without the help of a group or a counselor/therapist. Of course, self-help books should never be considered as substitutes for therapy, but they can be useful when psychotherapy is not needed, or as an adjunct to it. We both have had private practices in California and have worked in a variety of settings including street clinics, universities, school social work settings, and psychiatric clinics. From having co-taught classes and co-led groups, we are motivated by the need for a book to help people who want to grow, and to find an approach to their sexual relationships beyond contraception, security guards, HIV tests, sexual harassment suits, and all the protective devices that are being touted today.

On a personal note, we are both in long term loving marriages. We wish you well on your voyage through this book, and as you sail through troubled waters to loving relationships.

Barbara Childers and Eugenie G. Wheeler,
March 1996

CHAPTER 1

THE PURSUIT OF HAPPINESS

The winds and waves are always on the side of the ablest navigators.

Edward Gibbon

The Decline and Fall of the Roman Empire

What is a "loving relationship?" What does a loving relationship look like to you? What is your perception of a happy sexual relationship? Is it long term? Is it short term and dynamic, without the need for commitment? Is it a marital relationship? Is companionship more or less important than sexual ecstacy?

Your first thought might be "When I find a partner I can love and trust" or "When I enjoy sex more with my spouse." Maybe it is "When I am comfortable with my body" or "When I attract partners that are good for me, instead of 'losers,' when I know how to assure that I'm not taking any risks regarding AIDS, or any other sexually transmitted disease." Whatever your vision of "sexual happiness" you need to become more clear about your goals, before you begin to pursue them. Do the choices you have made so far move you in the direction you really want to go? Whatever you do today is definitely a part of where you are headed.

You begin this journey by making a clear, conscious decision that you want to respond to your highest and best self in charting your course. For most men and women, an over-riding goal is to be happy, to know what their partner wants without being expected to read his/her mind. Both sexes want to have fun together, to be able to expect fairness and consideration and some level of loyalty that, like all the other qualities, can be discussed. Let's look first at that illusive notion, happiness.

DO YOU LOOK FOR HAPPINESS IN ANOTHER?

What will your sexual happiness look like once you find it? Have you taken time to figure out how you will know when you are there? If not, it is apt to be like the carrot on a stick in front of the donkey. No matter how far you go, or how fast you travel, it will always be just out of your reach.

Perhaps you can conjure up your image of a perfect sexual partner, a perfect parent for your children, an ideal friend and companion. Of course, you realize, no one is perfect, but you want to find someone who comes close enough to your image for you to make it work.

There are dangers in this approach. One, if you find someone that seems to fit your ideal, then every time this person doesn't measure up, you will likely feel anger, frustration, and resentment. You might devalue yourself for picking the wrong person.

Don't be hard on yourself for choosing unwisely, but don't decide that you can change this other person, either. A nautical story gives an example of what can happen when you are determined to change the other person's behavior:

16

A large battleship is moving forcefully ahead one dark night, shining it's cruising lights, when the captain sees a small light straight ahead. He announces on his radio: "bear starboard." A voice comes back, "bear port." Somewhat angered, he responds: "This is a lead Navy ship, bear starboard!" The same voice comes back, "You bear port!" At this point the Admiral of the battleship gets on the radio and announces, "This is Admiral Strong in command. I demand that you bear starboard!" The voice comes back, "This is a lighthouse, bear port."

By taking charge of yourself, instead of trying to change others, you are much more likely to have smooth sailing into the kind of companionship and relationship that you want in your life.

Another danger is that when you look for happiness in what the other person is or does, you have given away your personal power. You place the power to make you happy in someone else's hands. Then you are likely to blame this person, who may have no idea of what went wrong. The very act of blaming is the act of giving away your power. This begins to look like the victim syndrome, where you are at the mercy of another person's actions.

A final danger may be the most important one. While you are focusing outside yourself, you are more likely to miss what is going on inside of you. Inside is where you will find the answers to what it takes to make you happy. It is where you will find the ghosts or patterns of your past that may be getting in your way. It is also where you need to focus to develop the paths and skills you need to help you get to your own personal place of happiness and inner peace.

17

LOOKING WITHIN

Your successful journey begins with your looking inside. Inside you carry everything that you have ever learned about sex, about love, about relationships, and about yourself. You carry the consequences of everything that has ever happened to you. This colors the view you have of everything outside of yourself. If happiness is a treasure chest, you are the keeper of the key.

DO YOU RISE TO YOUR CHALLENGES?

Are you still "waiting for the right man or woman to come along," or are you looking at what you may be doing that interferes with your own growth sexually? Is your lack of self-esteem reflected in poor choices of partners? Are you afraid to say "no" even when your health is at stake? Are your expectations too low, too high, or realistic? Do you isolate yourself, thus hindering any opportunity to find suitable partners? Or is your anxiety coming out as aggressiveness that drives others away? Have you found a way to ask whether a partner has been tested for AIDS?

Address your personal issues of sexuality as challenges instead of problems. When you focus on a problem you look to the past. You examine past mistakes or traumas. When you talk about a challenge, you are looking to the future. When you take on a challenge, you may use what you have learned in your past, but you are neither identified by it nor locked into it. You are moving forward in a conscious direction.

When you focus on a problem, it is easy to fall victim to the belief that you are the problem. When you focus on a challenge, you become a major part of the solution. Accepting a challenge means taking responsibility for change. Any issue is a complex combination of many factors. Instead of focusing on self-blame, look at yourself in relationship to the factors. Then examine the fit between you and the other factors. What are the areas where change can happen and you can help it to happen as you approach this challenge?

As you think about your personal goals and aspirations as a sexual being, and reflect on past experiences, both positive and negative, you will begin to identify specific areas of challenge. It's healthy to acknowledge that you have unresolved issues, that perhaps you have not taken adequate care of yourself. Demand of yourself that you identify what your issues are, and begin to claim your power by taking charge of your personal life.

Many factors may contribute to prolonging the time it will take for you to make your desired changes. Be on the alert for distractors such as denial, keeping too busy, "numbing out," or other avoidance techniques.

SET YOUR GOALS FOR A LOVING RELATIONSHIP

We are all sexual beings. How you view your sexuality can influence what you wear, what you eat (or don't eat), and what you buy. It also has a powerful influence on your self-esteem.

When sexuality or sexual energy enters into your relationships, it can be clear and direct, or subtle and circuitous. It can be invited or invasive. You can seek it, or it can catch you by surprise. The experience can be ecstatic or devastating. Whatever your experience, you want to feel good about the way you acted and reacted. That's a basic goal.

When setting goals, it helps to state them in specific terms that can be achieved. For example, because of past experience of abuse, Gina felt sexually inhibited, and shy. One of her goals was "to be more loving." This is stated as a process instead of as a specific accomplishment so she didn't know how to begin. It was more helpful when she restated her goal in specific terms as, "To initiate physical play with my partner at least once a week." It also has key qualities of a good goal; it is not only specific but also clear, and measurable. She can easily tell whether or not she has achieved it.

Define a reasonable time frame as a test for your goals. For example, Tom wanted to be more assertive, but knew he had many fears to overcome. He allowed himself three months to take an assertive training class and build his skills and confidence before he tried them on the person who interested him.

WHAT IS MOST IMPORTANT TO YOU?

What are the ingredients of loving sexual relationships? Fidelity? Good sex? The potential of being a good parent? A sense of humor? Loyalty? Willingness to...? You fill in the blanks. A helpful question to ask is, "Under what conditions would a relationship work for me?" If you know what is negotiable, and what are fixed values on your part, you can avoid false starts and misunderstandings.

Along with the issue of power, and the importance of good communication, in couple counseling five areas of concern that come up frequently are: sex, money, in-laws, religion, and child management. In this era of AIDS and other sexually transmitted diseases, it's necessary to add health to the list of most mentioned factors. So be aware of your values and needs in relation to all of these issues.

HEALTH

Disease can wreck any loving relationship. Of course, hardships can also strengthen bonds, but usually only if there is mutual trust and concern.

After Christine went through an unwanted divorce she went through a period of promiscuity before she recovered and began her new life as a responsible, single woman. When she started dating John, she couldn't bear to tell him about her past, including the fact that she had contracted herpes.

When the truth came to light, John said that he couldn't trust Christine, and broke off their relationship. He felt that if Christine had been honest from the beginning, they might have continued on. With medical help the health risks could have been minimized and the condition managed.

Now the importance of not only getting medical care, but also of being open about it with a sexual partner, is crucial. Physical and emotional aspects of your relationships are at stake.

EQUALITY

For most people, sexual happiness is having your and your partner's needs met, in an equal partnership, where neither feels used, dominated, or taken for granted. Arguments about sex and money are often based on power issues. Who is "supposed to do" what?

Eric, a minister, was hurt and appalled when Betty Anne expected him to help with the laundry, errands, and cooking. Betty Anne felt betrayed and put upon when Eric expected her to serve as laundress, errand girl, and cook. Their expectations stemmed from their exposure to the roles their parents played.

Eric's father, a Bishop, had been waited on hand and foot by all the women in his family all his life. It was felt by his family that it would be beneath his dignity, and bad for his image, to work in the kitchen or do menial tasks.

Betty Anne had been raised in a wealthy, "genteel Southern" household where she was considered a "belle" and never expected to work at all.

Since Eric and Betty Anne came from different backgrounds with different expectations, they had to redefine roles, and negotiate before they attained the equal, loving relationship they envisioned.

21

Do you see sexual equality as freedom to initiate intercourse, or to say "no?" Or freedom to have an "open" relationship where partners are free to have outside affairs? Hearts have been broken when definitions of trust and equality are different and aren't clarified.

SEXUAL COMMUNICATION

Most people agree that good communication is essential for a good relationship, but have difficulty in defining what constitutes good communication. Sometimes it helps to look at couple communication on three levels: verbal, affectional, and sexual. If one partner wants more affection while the other wants more frequent intercourse, it may be negotiable. Certainly it's essential that each know what he/she wants, and that each be able to express it.

Assumptions that your lover should be able to read your mind must go if you want to develop mutual understanding and mutual satisfaction. A sound criteria in assessing a relationship is whether you can talk about your feelings, express your needs verbally and non-verbally, and negotiate differences.

With good sexual communication skills you can reduce your fears, such as the fear of pregnancy and the ensuing responsibility, fear of herpes (or any other physical problem), or date rape (and other kinds of sexual assault). You will be less vulnerable and less likely to find yourself in the victim role. You will be less likely to end up with a partner that is a threat to your health or your very life.

COMPANIONSHIP

What does companionship mean to you? Does it include day-to-day "did you sleep well?" kind of togetherness? Going to a basketball game together? Playing and praying together? How do you see sexual intercourse? As release of tension? As a spiritual experience? As a way to feel close to another person and express your love for them? As a fun, playful activity?

If companionship is important to you, are you referring to sexual companionship, or other kinds as well? The kind of companionship you want may be hard to define because there are many different kinds. You may or may not be roommates, or share financially, intellectually, or spiritually, but if you do you're aware of how impossible it is to separate these kinds and levels of companionship from sexual companionship.

Following is an example of how communication about recreation baffled one married couple:

Jeff and Debbie were pleased when they reached agreement that they both needed more leisure time. They felt that accord about leisure was an important ingredient in their marriage.

Jeff called his buddy and said, "Guess what? Debbie and I have had a talk and I can go on hunting trips after all." Debbie told her mother that Jeff had "come around" so they would be spending a lot of their weekends with her and Dad. When Jeff and Debbie first realized that recreation meant something entirely different to each of them, they became frustrated and discouraged until they learned to compromise.

If your partner wants different kinds of activities, recreational and otherwise, than you do, don't be too quick to judge the companionship factor as hopeless. Instead, look at it from a position of the strengths in your relationship, and how your differences might alternate or complement each other. Then your differences may be seen as complementarity instead of as unsurmountable obstacles. Expanding your view and/or some negotiation might be easier than finding another sexual partner.

Recreation can be individual, as a couple, and socializing with others. You need all three kinds for balance in your life. Discuss these three aspects with your partner and decide which of these types of recreation needs more focus, or time.

FINANCIAL ISSUES

To set your goals you need to know what's important to you in the financial area, as well. For example if equality is one of your values, how do you see it being achieved in financial matters? Will you have separate bank accounts, chip in equal amounts, or pro-rate according to income? How much accountability are you willing to tolerate?

Expectations in this area, too, need to be clarified:

The therapist was doing pre-marriage counseling. She asked Ethel how much money they would need for her to feel financially secure in her marriage with Tony. She was thoughtful, then estimated that about $1,000 in savings and $500 in a checking account would be minimum.

Tony's response was, "If no more than one item was repossessed a month, I'd feel O.K."

It would be difficult to reconcile such divergent expectations and needs. They decided to break their engagement thus making good use of counseling.

Equal partnerships will be easier to achieve and maintain when equal pay for equal work is part of our society's values. Women's lower salaries and wages make them, in some families, responsible for more than a fair share of household tasks.

IN-LAWS

In-laws are a potential source of strength or of disaster. If either partner is excessively dependent on their family of origin, they are not ready for a mature, adult relationship:

David was so tired of Winona's threats that she was going to go home to her mother that he finally responded, "Go ahead."

Winona got so tired of David's disparaging remarks about her house work in comparison to his mother's that she encouraged him, too, to go back home til he grew up.

RELIGION

Religion is often an area of concern or conflict for couples. You may not be aware of the impact it has on your intimacy.

Gail and Terry were very much in love. They decided to move in together to save money and to have more time with each other. Gail continued to resist intercourse, believing it should be saved for marriage. Terry loved her very much and was willing to wait. He believed it was a question of her building enough trust in him. But that was not the issue. She was hurt that he didn't ask her to marry him.

It took counseling before they talked enough about the issue to reach understanding. Terry thought that if he was gentle and patient enough, Gail would lose her fear, and make love. He was waiting for this level of trust before he asked her to marry him. Since they had never really discussed it, he didn't realize that her attitude was based on a strict religious belief and had nothing to do with how much she trusted him.

CHILD MANAGEMENT

If a couple cannot resolve their differences and come to mutual understanding and policies regarding the rearing of his/her, and their children, their relationship is in jeopardy, and the children suffer. These issues hit at the very core of a person's philosophy about family values which include sexual values. They are complex and their resolution is a must in setting goals for any loving, long term relationship that involves children.

By reading this book you have taken a first step toward achieving your relationship goals. Rather than following someone else's agenda you're taking responsibility for building your own. You cannot eliminate concern about your sexual relationships, but if you clarify what you want, and set your goals wisely, worry won't block you from achieving them.

To rise to your challenges you need knowledge, techniques, and strengths. You can learn to recognize your potential for building solid, loving relationships, while diplomatically avoiding unwanted connections. You can also recognize the "red flags" or indicators that a relationship might be destructive.

Your clarity in articulating who you are and what you want, makes it easier for the other person in the relationship to be more clear and honest with you. It helps you to know when there is honesty and when there is manipulation. You can learn to recognize game-playing and be more able to work toward a safe, equal partnership. Being clear helps you to hold your own in delicate, or dangerous, sexually charged situations, and to be free to choose your degree of intimacy, and with whom.

As you develop skills and move beyond negotiation to healthy, balanced loving relationships, you can claim your sexual self, with all its multiple dimensions of strength, playfulness, power, and joy.

TO DO LIST

1. Find a way to remind yourself on a regular basis that you deserve fulfillment and to enjoy your sexual self. This could be a note on your bathroom mirror, in your purse or wallet, or in your car. Commit to yourself that you are going to take steps in this direction.

2. Keep track of how much time you spend, making yourself happy, on a weekly basis:

- In individual recreation (without your partner), such as with your women/men's softball team, little theater group, etc.
- With your relatives? With your in-laws?
- With your partner?
- With other people, socially?

Now that you have identified your recreational pattern, consider which aspects you'd like to maximize or minimize.

3. Consider your financial needs and how much financial autonomy you require. How much financial accountability is acceptable to you? Do you want a separate bank account? One joint account and a jointly written budget? Monthly conferences for financial planning? Are you willing to take over most of the responsibility? Are you willing to delegate it?

4. If you have children, or if your partner does, discuss your theories of child rearing. If there are serious differences, would it be necessary to you for you and your partner to get family counseling?

Your answers to these questions will help you set specific goals for loving relationships. Your goals will lay the foundation upon which to build your sexual self-contract.

Sexual Challenges

CHAPTER 2

TROUBLED WATERS

The sexual environment throughout the world today is in a confused if not a chaotic state. To achieve a loving relationship many dangers need to be avoided and hurdles overcome. Some of the proliferating troubles are highlighted below.

The obstacles can be threats of violent storms like AIDs or sexual assault. Some of the shoals in troubled waters can be minor ripples, like shyness at asking someone for a date for the first time, or for the first time in many years. Most of the seemingly less traumatic sexual challenges are also significant in that if they are not dealt with appropriately, they will escalate into major hazards to loving relationships. Some indicators to look for are verbal and emotional abuse, jealousy, and over-dependency.

SEXUALLY TRANSMITTED DISEASES

Sexually transmitted diseases, or STDs, are flourishing in the United States, some at their highest levels ever. Teenagers and young adults are the primary victims of

STDs, which, in turn, boost the risk of contracting the human immunodeficiency virus, becoming infertile, or giving birth to babies with health problems. One in five adult Americans carries some type of viral STD such as herpes, which are not curable to date. When the curable bacterial STDs such as syphilis, gonorrhea, and chlamydia are included, Americans have at least a one-in-four lifetime chance of contracting a sexually transmitted disease. The alarming news is that although the HIV threat may be convincing some to practice safe sex, it is not reaching or effecting the behavior of many others.

AIDS

AIDS is the number one sexually transmitted disease and the major cause of death among Americans aged twenty-five to forty-four according to the Centers for Disease Control and Prevention. In 1994 there were 30,000 AIDS orphans in New York City, 10,000 in New Jersey, and the number of youngsters orphaned by AIDS could more than double by the year 2000 to 3.7 million worldwide. The lifetime costs of treating someone with HIV/AIDS in the United States is $119,000. The federal government spends $2.95 per capita annually on AIDS prevention.

But condom use is limited. Even with the health problems we face today only an estimated fourteen percent of sexually active unmarried heterosexuals who are not in monogamous relationships use condoms each and every time.

Paula, recently divorced at age 48, is suffering from the loss of her husband after a long-term marriage. He married his secretary. Moreover, Paula is grieving the death of her son who died of AIDS. Among her fears is the possibility that she's never again going to have any masculine companionship in her life. Bemoaning that she didn't have the social skills to date again — she hasn't had a date in many years — she says she wouldn't know how to act. She's afraid she might get AIDS, that she might have the HIV virus herself from a blood transfusion she got before blood was checked for it. She's aware that losing her son to AIDS heightens her anxiety, but that insight doesn't make her apprehension go away.

UNPROTECTED SEX AND UNWANTED PREGNANCIES

Unwanted pregnancies are on the rise. Although the rate of births among unmarried teens has risen substantially over the past several decades, most non-marital births occur to women who are twenty years old or older.

The life-altering and tragic consequences of unprotected sex are under-reported. The reality of an unwanted pregnancy and the wrenching decisions associated with it change lives irrevocably. Loss of loved ones from AIDS and fear of AIDS wreak havoc in many families:

Sue, at 20, is unmarried, pregnant, and deserted by the alcoholic, putative father. She returns to her parents' home broke, without skills or resources. She has AIDS, is desperate, and her parents' lifestyle and security are disrupted for years to come.

SEXUAL VIOLENCE

Violence in relationships is on the increase. Every forty five seconds in the United States a woman is sexually assaulted. Each year more than seven hundred thousand suffer the wounds, psychic shock and humiliation of sexual assault. The president of the American Medical Association, Dr. Lonnie Bristow, called for greater public awareness of an "epidemic growing at an alarming rate and traumatizing the women and children of our nation."

In 1993 twenty seven percent of the females killed in California died at the hands of their mates or former mates according to the state Bureau of Criminal Statistics. An AMA report states that in three-fourths of all sexual assaults, the victims, ninety-five percent of them female, know the attackers as friends, acquaintances, intimate partners or family members. These associations often stand in the way of the assaults being reported. The Los Angeles Police Department handles sixty five thousand domestic violence calls a year. Battery is the greatest cause of injury to women nationwide prompting more emergency room visits than auto accidents, rapes, and muggings combined.

VERBAL AND EMOTIONAL ABUSE

Sometimes what appears to be verbal abuse is just "dumping" which means unloading frustrations on you because you're handy. Know when you're not the target, and get away from such ranting.

One reason why emphasis on good sexual communication is so important is because verbal abuse can, and frequently does, escalate into violence. The first step in learning the skills of stopping this form of abuse is awareness of what's happening. Verbal abuse can come from men or women and can take the form of mean jokes, vicious belittling, false blame and bullying. Or it can consist of disparaging remarks like, "If I left you nobody else would want you... No one else would put up with you." Bullying can be intimidation, harassment, hazing, pestering. Some college campus groups have developed the following classifications:

Withholding: This can be verbal or non-verbal. They don't say what they mean, deny what you say, and say, "I don't know" when they do know. They act dissatisfied with your sexual performance, but won't discuss it.

Projection: They say things like, "You're jumping to conclusions, you blow everything out of proportion, you're making mountains out of mole hills, you think you know everything..."

Covert: This is subtle psychological abuse that is difficult to come to terms with because they'll say, "I was just kidding. You have no sense of humor," or they'll make veiled threats, or they'll manipulate through devious verbal coercion. They will lure you on to sexual experimentation that is beyond your comfort zone, then put you down for being "over-sexed."

JEALOUSY

Jealousy can be a minor or a major threat, especially in immature relationships. Young women often look for someone to take care of them, and misinterpret jealousy and over-control as flattering. Often they have little awareness or skill in picking up on signals that are warning signs of potential violence.

Victor insisted that Alice take someone with her when she went to the market because he was afraid that she might flirt with the bag boys. The rest of the time she was to stay home. He was even jealous of Alice's girlfriends. These limitations were O.K. with Alice while their child was still an infant. But when she went to a parenting class, and he lurked in the hallway to be sure that there were no men around, she started to rebel. The more she rebelled, the more he tightened his control. Finally she left him. In the end, he lost her and custody of their baby.

When jealousy is the problem, marriage counseling can help. Jealousy is based on insecurity, so the challenge is to improve Victor's self-esteem, and help them both develop mutual trust.

Dottie was so possessive of Harry that he felt as if he was in a vice. She checked his collars for lipstick stains, questioned him endlessly about his where-

abouts, and telephoned his office when he said he had to work late to be sure he was there. Harry had had it, but decided instead of blowing up at her, or thinking, "Well, she's going to mistrust me anyway, I might as well do as I please," he tried to negotiate a plan to build a more solid relationship. But Dottie's insecurity was so great and her jealousy so intense that he finally said, "I couldn't take it any more. I took a hike. Even God couldn't meet that woman's needs."

If you feel that your jealousy is excessive, discuss it with your partner, and try to build trust. If you don't succeed on your own, consider getting therapy.

OVER-DEPENDENCY

Anyone who derives their identity totally from attachment to another person risks losing a sense of his/her self when the relationship ends. Adolescents don't have a monopoly on identity crises. Since there are five widows for every widower in the United States, and the number of men who leave their wives for younger women continues to rise, many ex-wives are in a position of having to remake their lives in middle age. "One of the cruelest parts of being an 'out-of-work' wife," writes columnist Anna Quindlen "is the loss of identity. One woman says that what finally did her in was the name, the 'Mrs. John Smith' on another woman's stationery."

Quindlen tells of an extreme case, one where a wife gave her all, abdicated tending to her own needs in favor of subordination to her husband. Betty Broderick, serving a long prison sentence for the murders of her ex-husband and his second wife, had seen her husband through professional school, skimped and saved in the early lean years, and car pooled the kids. She worked long and hard at wifehood, and then her husband left her. She went berserk, incapable of building a new life because the job she had always counted on was to be Mrs. Dan Broderick. Quindlen concludes with the thought that Princess Diana, "once an emblem of romantic love, has now become a representative of how horribly things sometimes turn out when a woman hitches all her hopes to one man's star, an object lesson in the need for self-reliance and a life of one's own."

The extent of STDs, violence, verbal and emotional abuse, jealousy and over-dependency, is an indication of the importance of charting your course with care to avoid the risks of sexual diseases and violence. You want to be a giving person, and to enjoy a loving relationship, but not at the expense of taking care of yourself; not at the expense of equality. Fortunately it's never too late to experiment with new roles and build new identities.

TO DO LIST

1. Ask yourself the following questions:

- Am I **giving in too much**, or being controlled by my dates (or partner)?

- Am I **giving out too much**, in the sense of putting others' needs ahead of my own?

- Am I **giving up**, or withdrawing, because I think I can't handle sexual situations?

2. List one or more areas of personal concern that you want to be sure to address when you develop your sexual self-contract.

CHAPTER 3

CHART YOUR SEXUAL
SELF-CONTRACT

The contracting process can shift the focus of atten-
tion from fault-finding to problem-solving... toward
positive changes in behavior.
Writing Behavioral Contracts
DiRisi, William J., and Butz, George
Research Press, 1975

The authors believe that you can best achieve your goal
of a safe, loving relationship by preparing a sexual self-
contract that helps you get past the dangers and over the
hurdles described in the last chapter. Your contract will
help you define what you want, develop the insights, and
acquire the skills you need to reach your goal.

You can "resolve" to act in certain ways, but that
resolve is not going to stick when the pressure is on unless
your resolution is backed up with reinforcement if you
follow through, and/or contingencies if you don't. If you
implement a part of your contract you need to find a way
to reward yourself. If you fail to keep to what you've
committed to, you need to have a preplanned activity as a

result. For example, if you have unprotected sex after promising yourself that you won't, you need to have a built in clause that you will then be tested for AIDS, or take some other appropriate action as a consequence.

DEVELOPING A SEXUAL SELF-CONTRACT

Have you ever been in an intimate situation and felt ambivalent about how far to go? Were there times when you felt out of control, like being at sea without a rudder? Have you acquiesced to what someone else wanted or needed because you weren't able to assert your needs clearly? At such times, wrong choices can hurt you or someone else. Much of this can be avoided with a clear, strong, personal **sexual self-contract**. Such a self-contract can rescue you from ambivalence and indecision. For Example:

Kathy:

> *As a college junior, Kathy was eager to make friends. At the dorm dance she did not make a strong connection with anyone. She was relieved when her roommate, Sarah, asked her to join her and two guys for pizza after the dance. There was more beer drinking than Kathy was used to, but she was having fun. When it was time to leave and she stood up, she knew she had far too much to drink. Later, at the guys' apartment, she was in no condition to resist her date's sexual advances. The next morning her memory was vague, but she knew they had sex. She was mortified. This was not how she had wanted to begin her junior year.*

Perhaps you've returned home after a social event, and were angry with yourself for drinking too much. Or you went on a double date to please a friend, and regretted it because your friend wanted to be sexual with his/her partner, and you didn't.

Pam and Celeste:

Pam's and Celeste's situation shows that it isn't only young people who fall into patterns that result in their being down on themselves.

In a women's support group Pam and Celeste, both divorcees in their forties, discovered that they had similar sex patterns and were both worried about them. Pam said, "I plan not to have sex until I get to know the man very well, but somehow I always succumb. I always think that somehow this time it's going to be different." "Tell me about it," responded Celeste. "I am disgusted with myself over and over again. I think it's because I haven't recovered from my divorce, but that excuse is getting old."

A sexual self-contract could help both these women integrate their principles into their lifestyles. They would feel a stronger sense of control and self-worth as a result.

Does guilt interfere with your love life? Guilt for thoughts or feelings that are involuntary? This is a hard one to talk about, and can be immobilizing.

Niles:

Niles was having a problem because he rejected his wife after her mastectomy. He was ashamed of himself for feeling the way he did. Moreover, he was tempted to have an affaire. He was consumed by guilt, even though he hadn't "done" anything wrong.

Even when things were going well, have you ever felt trapped by your own values and beliefs? Two principles that you value highly might come into conflict when you find strong loving feelings stirring, and it wasn't part of your "plan."

Jim:

Jim planned to stay emotionally uninvolved for his freshman year of college and stay focused on his studies. Although intelligent, he had not applied himself well in high school. His grades would have kept him out of college if his test scores had not been high. In his Math class he made friends with Terry, another intelligent and industrious student. They became study partners. It wasn't part of either of their plans, but they soon found themselves attracted to each other, and then romantically involved. Jim would make plans, but Terry would distract him when they were together.

WHAT IS A SEXUAL SELF-CONTRACT?

Your sexual self-contract is a pre-prescribed set of rules you set for yourself to direct your behavior like a compass at sea. It's a strategy to help you reach loving relationships, to prevent unwanted, distasteful experiences along the way, and to increase the likelihood of positive experiences. It is your clear statement of who you are as a sexual being, how you want to present yourself, and how you choose to respond to others. It states with whom, and in what ways, you choose to share your sexual energy.

One distinction between a sexual self-contract and other forms of agreements and contracts is that this one is **by** and **for** you. Usually contracts are between two different people or groups, both of whom have something to gain from the contract. Your own sexual self-contract provides for just you — your functioning in social or sexual situations. The functioning it recommends will not be illegal, or too much at variance with local customs.

Consider Legal Factors

Confusion and mixed messages about sexual policy are not limited to private musings. You find contradictions in public law and legal practice as well. For example, an act of sexual aggression is a criminal act, yet different states define "sexual aggression" differently, and enforcement policies also vary. Other examples of inconsistencies can be seen in age requirements, restrictions on sexual behaviors, etc.

Consider Cultural Factors

In addition to laws governing sexual policy, community or cultural values and practices can wield strong control. Cultural and family customs dictate the age at which dating can start, and provide rituals to accompany different stages of intimacy. For example in some countries premarital sex is accepted. At the point of engagement, the couple shares a bedroom in the parents' home, and an elaborate breakfast is brought to the room the next morning. Practices may vary from country to country, or from one home to the next. People differ in how much they accept the values and dictates taught to them by their parents and their culture of origin.

You may feel that kissing in public is acceptable, but you may live in a senior community where it is frowned upon so strongly that you choose not to. If you're a hugger, and believe that hugs draw people closer together and dilute pain, you may choose not to hug in certain situations. If people become rigid if you even look like you're thinking about a hug, you'll desist. No matter what your personal policy, you probably won't do much hugging in that kind of group. Any touching in public is taboo in many cultures. Being sensitive to the policies and practices of those around you can help you avoid embarrassment and help you make friends. You need to design your sexual self-contract in ways that are appropriate to the environment you're in if you want it to work well for you.

Once you allow for the legal constraints, and are sensitive to local practices, your sexual self-contract can be under your control. Getting these boundaries clear is an important first step.

Other Factors

With a clear sexual self-contract you will know when you are reacting to another's agenda as opposed to acting upon your own agenda. This can make the difference between feeling victimized, and feeling self-confident and in control.

Remember that you cannot control the plans or behavior of others. Neither can you take the blame or the credit for how they respond to you. The good news is that by your behavior, words, and choices you **can** influence another. Mutual satisfaction will come about when you teach others how to treat you. By observing your carefully created sexual self-contract, you will be more likely to walk away from sexual encounters feeling good about yourself. Even if you reject someone, that person will be more likely to retain self-esteem and leave the relationship with their respect for you intact.

Self-knowledge

I'll walk where my own nature would be leading —
It vexes me to choose another guide.

Emily Bronte, "Stanzas"1850

A significant first step in achieving loving relationships is to know yourself; to define who you are. You grew up with mixed messages about what is good or proper. You may have accepted a policy that is difficult to follow. The trouble is that it isn't **your** policy. It's someone else's that you have adopted.

Do you know what drives you? What is it that you really want? Once you set a policy that is yours, it will be easier to follow than one imposed on you.

Establishing Your Rights & Responsibilities

I'm not afraid of storms, for I'm learning how to sail my ship.

Louisa May Alcott, *Little Women* 1868

As you prepare to develop your contract with yourself, consider the following **affirmations:**

- I have a right and a responsibility to determine my own personal plan for responding to sexual challenges.

- I will develop a sexual self-contract with myself that enhances my self-esteem and works for my best interest as a healthy, happy, sexual being.

- I will choose with whom I share information about my sexual self-contract.

- My sexual self-contract may not be changed while I am in a sexually charged or sexually challenging situation.

EXAMPLES OF CONTRACTS THAT WORKED

Example 1. Kathy (who you met at the beginning of this chapter) decided to forgive herself and make a new start toward keeping control of herself and sticking to her principles. Part of her contract stated that she would limit her drinking to two beers or two glasses of wine on any one date. She would not go to a date's apartment until she'd been out with him several times, and she'd find out more about a blind date before she went out with him.

Example 2. Pam defined a "five date delay" policy for herself. No sex until after the fifth date.

Celeste chose abstinence until marriage. Both felt armed with contracts based on their own principles; on who they wanted to be and what kind of relationships they wanted.

Example 3. After the idea of a contract was introduced to Niles he decided to take some action to resolve the difficulty before turning away from his marriage. His plan involved consultation with his doctor, and a visit with a close friend in a distant city whose wife had similar surgery. Based on the advice he received, he made a contract that provided for his gradually becoming more affectionate, in small easy-to-take steps, as a way to desensitize himself in relation to his wife's physical loss. If this didn't work, his contract called for his getting into therapy. In time, however, as he implemented his plan, he and his wife became closer than ever, and did not need counseling.

Example 4. Jim and Terry, his study buddy, found that they both felt the same way. They both wanted the relationship, but felt the same way about the importance of their academic goals. They were able to talk about it easily, and decided to design a joint sexual self contract. Their contract makes room for both of them to pursue a high standard of scholarship, while nurturing their relationship.

CREATING YOUR SEXUAL SELF-CONTRACT

As you develop your contract, remember that it is a working document. It doesn't have to be perfect the first time; it's merely a first draft. The most important part is to **do** it. Get it down on paper. It's O.K. to peek at the samples and guidelines at the end of this chapter.

You will be adding to your draft as you read through the book. When you reach the end, you will see how you can revise and update it. Once you have a draft, it will be easier to correct or adjust it. Some guidelines to follow:

- Find a time and space where you can be alone, and feel safe.

  Don't do this at your boyfriend's, girlfriend's, or parents' house if you don't want to be influenced by them. Do it where you feel you are in charge.

- Get comfortable, with pen and paper handy.

  Once your creativity starts, you don't want to be distracted looking for something to write on!

- Think of at least three things you love and appreciate about yourself. Notice how these qualities feel. You might want to write them as a kind of preamble to your contract. For example, "I am an honest and caring person." Or, "I am intelligent and creative." Or, "I'm sensitive to the feelings of others."

  It's important to work on your sexual self-contract when you're feeling good about yourself so that your decisions will not be based on guilt or pleasing others. It needs to be based on honoring who you really are and how you want to be.

- Write down whatever ideas come to your mind that might develop into guidelines. Write as many ideas as you can.

  Brainstorm! This is your chance to explore all possible options. If it helps, recreate in your mind past situations that you wish you had handled differently. What would have helped? (i.e. "I will limit myself to two alcoholic drinks in any 4 hour period.") Think of possible scenarios and how you would like to handle them if they arise. What could have made it a positive experience? (i.e. "When I go to a social event and don't know many people, I will introduce myself to at least three people in the first hour.")

- Include health issues.

Brainstorm some more about your choices re: contraception, STD protection, keeping fit. (i.e. I'll be HIV tested if... I'll ask if my partner has been...)

- Be specific.

Generalizations are difficult to apply and evaluate later. Be clear about place, time, amount, and any other specifications you need. (i.e. "If I am in a group of three or more...")

- Say it in a positive mode if possible.

When you say what you don't want ("I don't want to have sex on a first date," or "I won't go out with married women,") the mind can play tricks, especially under stress, and you are more likely to do what you said ("...have sex on a first date," "go out with a married woman.") It is far more effective if you describe what you do want, ("I'll keep my pants on/zippered up on a first date," "I'll check out marital status, date single women.")

- Sleep on it.

Once you have written as many ideas and guidelines as you can think of, take a break. Set it aside. Go for a walk, or distract yourself in some other way. The best is to "sleep on it" and look at it again the next day.

- Refine your list.

Review what you have written. Make additions or deletions. Combine, strengthen, reorganize or rewrite until you feel good about what you have written.

- Practice.

Imagine scenarios that you might experience. Use a mirror. Tell yourself what you plan to tell your partner. Rephrase it or try it several different ways until you are comfortable hearing it. You may feel foolish at first, but you will feel stronger when the actual experience presents itself - and it will be worth it.

- Commit to your Contract.

Sign your contract. Commit to yourself that you will not make any changes without giving them the same careful consideration you gave when you wrote it. Realize that anyone who tries to get you to go against your own best interest is probably not someone you want to have in your life.

Once you have developed the first draft of your sexual self-contract, you can watch for opportunities to put it into practice. Ideally, you will be able to practice it in situations that are not of major consequence until you get comfortable with it. Choose one of your new policies that seems the easiest, and try it first. Small successes will give you more courage to hold to your self-respect in more difficult encounters. Whatever your experiences with it, you'll be in a better position to make sound revisions when you've tried it out.

Note the reinforcers and contingencies in the sample contracts on the following pages, and develop your own in relation to each clause. If you elect to write a joint contract with your partner, design it to be mutually reinforcing. For example, if your partner agrees to reinforce you for taking some responsibility in some area — housework or finances, for instance — then you will respond to a request of his/hers to reinforce him/her.

SEXUAL SELF-CONTRACT

INTRODUCTION

1. I want a self-contract because..............

2. My Goals for a Loving Relationship are.......

SEXUAL SELF-AWARENESS

1. The kind of sexual relationship I desire is....

2. To acquire this kind of relationship I will...

3. To avoid mistakes I've made in the past I will...

4. I will develop a healthy balance between my sexual life and my individual growth by sustaining interest in.....and pursuing new interests such as...

COMMUNICATION

1. I will listen carefully to what a potential partner says concerning sexual values and preferences and ask the following questions at appropriate times...

2. I will express the following beliefs about sexual intimacy to my partner prior to sexual involvement...

3. To further improve my communication skills (verbal and non-verbal), I will respond with one of the following answers...

4. If someone expresses a desire to see more of me — and I'm not interested — I will respond with...

5. If I become involved in a relationship that does not feel right to me, I will take the following steps to end it in a non-confrontational, yet direct manner...

SAFE SEX

1. I will avoid the risk of contracting AIDS, STDs (or an unwanted pregnancy, if applicable) by taking the following preventive measures before I become sexually involved...

2. I will be prepared to deal with any kind of potential abuse by...

3. If I should have a traumatic experience, I will seek help from...

SELF-REINFORCEMENT

1. When I have implemented my sexual self-contract for (length of time to be determined), I will reward myself by...

2. If I should fail to follow through with these commitments, I will...

Signature.............

Date.....................

SAMPLE CONTRACT - WOMAN

INTRODUCTION

1. I want a self-contract because I'm insecure sexually and have difficulty in saying "no." I let sex-play go further than I want it to, and then regret it. Also, when I'm anxious I tend to eat too much and need to get control of my weight.

2. My goals for a loving relationship are: To share with a partner the same values, i.e. loyalty, trust, honesty, and monogamy. To be mutually supportive emotionally. To have mutual, but also separate goals/activities in regard to our social life. To share financial responsibility for running the kind of home, and recreational life that we both want.

A relationship in which we will plan for children in the future.

SEXUAL SELF-AWARENESS

1. In assessing my strengths and weaknesses I realize that my feelings about being overweight govern my sexual self-image.

My strengths: I'm a loyal friend and capable of developing the kind of relationship I want; of pulling my weight emotionally, sexually, financially, and in all the areas that are important to me.

My weaknesses include insecurity, not taking charge of my sexual and eating behaviors when my self-esteem is low.

2. I will take following steps to raise my self-esteem:

I will walk every day, eat sensibly, and join an exercise class. If I lose ten pounds in three months, I will reward myself with a new top. If I don't, I will join a weight loss program like Weight Watchers.

I will complete my contract including specific limits as to how far I will go in sexual encounters, and under what circumstances. I will use this contract as a way to stay in charge of my behavior. This will help me feel more in control, which, in turn, will raise my self-esteem.

COMMUNICATION

1. I will improve my listening skills by checking out with my partner what she/he meant to be sure I've understood the intent of what's been said. I'll note whether I'm talking most of the time, half the time, or less, in the conversations I have with my partner and others.

2. I will continue to raise my awareness of the sexual signals I send by noticing my gestures, being "mindful" of when I'm flirting, and getting feedback from a close friend about how I come across.

3. I will practice the two-step "No" when asked for small, non-sexual favors to prepare myself to stay in control in sexual situations, and to be able to "slow it down."

SAFE SEX

1. I will not tolerate verbal or emotional abuse. I will counter it successfully, get couple counseling, or end the relationship. I will avoid it by not dating strangers, picking up people in bars, or going on blind dates without high recommendations from people I trust.

2. At any sign of physical abuse, I will end the relationship.

3. I will have sexual intercourse only after I've had dates or been to social or other events with the potential partner a minimum of seven times, only if I've asked if s/he has been tested for AIDS and received a satisfactory reply, and only if a condom is used.

4. If I'm sexually assaulted I will get involved in some kind of counseling immediately.

SELF-REINFORCEMENT

1. I will keep a journal in connection with this contract to track my progress in implementing it, and also to keep track of when and what revisions I may want to consider.

I will make affirmations part of my journal starting with:

—I will develop affirmations to help me keep my self-esteem high, and to keep me on track.

—I am attractive and I'm losing weight. I'm confident and am building my self-esteem succesfully.

2. I will select someone to tell about my contract who will be understanding and will help me celebrate my successes. I will suggest that we have outings at monthly intervals as I succeed, and that we cancel them if I slip.

3. After six months of success, I will reward myself by buying a whole new, size smaller, sexy, wardrobe. If I don't succeed: no new clothes until I do.

Signature.................

Date........................

SAMPLE CONTRACT - MAN

INTRODUCTION

1. I need a contract I can use to remind myself that I have a lot to give in an intimate, loving relationship.

2. I need a sexual self-contract to also remind myself that it is not necessary to fit the Hollywood stereotype to be in a loving relationship.

3. My goal is to have an intimate, loving, sexual, relationship with some one who will love and trust me, and whom I can love and trust.

SEXUAL SELF-AWARENESS

1. Instead of trying to be something I'm not, I will take time to understand myself better.

2. As I focus on self-awareness, I'll build my self-esteem, trusting that I can find and keep a partner that will bring me joy.

3. I will read more about myths regarding size, athletic prowess in relation to sex, and other "Jock" values in order to counter them and my feelings of inferiority. I will trace where and when I internalized these false values for more insight and self-knowledge.

4. When I am in my "birthday suit" I will keep the level of my self-confidence just as high as it is when I'm in a business suit.

COMMUNICATION

1. I will work on communicating my likes, dislikes, and feelings directly and clearly, encouraging my partner to do the same. If I realize I have not done this, I'll correct it as soon as possible.

53

2. When I want to compliment a date, I'll look for qualities other than physical appearance to focus on.

SAFE SEX

1. I will insist on protecting both myself and my partner when we have sex. I will have protective devices with me, or not get involved.

2. When I'm sexually involved, I'll take responsibility for birth control, even if the woman says she is safe.

3. I will not have intercourse on a first date.

SELF-REINFORCEMENT

1. When I feel a need for healing, or to reward myself, I will set out one hour's worth of my favorite CD's. I'll put the phone on answer, and take that hour, uninterrupted, to stretch out on the couch and just listen. Then I'll take a shower and "wash away" any negativity I want to get rid of.

2. To reward myself for sticking to my contract for a six month period, I'll take a trip, hopefully with a partner, to a resort area for at least a week.

Signature............
Date...................

SAMPLE CONTRACT - COUPLE

INTRODUCTION

1. We want a sexual contract because we've both been in unsatisfactory relationships and we want to take preventive steps to avoid a repetition of some of the problems we've experienced in the past.

2. Our goals are the same: a loving relationship in which we share our lives and support each other in our individual as well as in our mutual pursuits.

SEXUAL SELF-AWARENESS

1. We love our playfulness, but if either is stressed and not in the mood for it, we will strive for open and honest expression of feelings without judgement or defensiveness.

COMMUNICATION

1. Every day we will take a few minutes to tell each other something that we have especially appreciated about our partner.

2. Any issues that arise between us, we will save to talk about when we are alone; not in front of friends or family.

3. We will not walk away from an unresolved issue without setting a time to work on it.

4. We acknowledge both our need and right for some alone time. We will communicate about this issue so that when one of us withdraws into a separate activity, or just wants to be alone, the other won't interpret this as rejection, and confusion won't result.

5. If we think our partner is upset with us, we will ask, and not guess or make assumptions. We will not make plans for each other without first getting consent.

6. We will have a weekly planning session to discuss financial issues, distribution of household chores, and recreational projects.

SAFE SEX

1. We will not indulge in unprotected sex.

2. Neither of us will have a sexual relationship with anyone else as long as we are living together and committed to each other.

REINFORCEMENT

1. We will have a "date," or "mini-celebration" weekly as a way of honoring our relationship and assuring that we will not take it, or each other for granted. This will reinforce our contract.

2. If we agree that we've kept to this contract, we'll continue our celebrations. If either of us feels we're failing, the other will agree to go for some kind of joint counseling.

Signed.......................

Signed.....................

Date......................

TO DO LIST

Review the draft of your contract. Check for the following:

1. Are the goals realistic and specific?

2. Are they doable, i.e., within your ability to achieve?

3. Is monitoring built in so you will review it at specified times?

4. Have you built in contingencies? For example, if you have difficulty with compliance, you will take time away from dating to rethink what you want in your contract, or you will see a counselor, or take some other action to help you get on track.

5. Have you also written in ways to reinforce yourself for your compliance? Note what's reinforcing to you — new clothes? Going to a ball game? Dinner at a special place? Treat yourself for your successes.

Put your draft of your sexual self-contract into practice remembering that this first attempt is just the beginning. Read on for information and ideas that will help you complete it and make it more useful to you.

Sexual Challenges

CHAPTER 4

MYTHS AND REALITY

We Live in a fantasy world, a world of illusion. The great task in life is to find reality.
Iris Murdoch, in Rachel Billington,
"Profile: Iris Murdoch"

Myths and misinformation you picked up as a child can generate a lot of confusing baggage that blocks your path to your goal of achieving loving relationships. Your contract will help you address them and correct them.

"Myth" has more than one meaning in our culture. When a myth is used in the traditional sense, as a story to explain some custom or phenomenon, it can serve to enhance relationships. Cultural myths may help keep beautiful, ancient traditions alive. They are the foundation for many rituals associated with sexual maturity or mating rites. They expand our imaginations and nourish our sexual fantasies. Who has not been charmed by myths or fairy tales of the loves of ancient heros and heroines and their heroic sacrifices for love? We encourage the use of this kind of myth to give both tradition and vision to healthy, loving relationships. However, it is the "fictitious story," or falsehood type of myth that is the focus of this chapter; the myths that can distort, block or even destroy opportunities for sexual joy and wholeness.

Myths of pursuing happiness, as mentioned in chapter one, pale in comparison to some of our common sexual myths. "Women with big breasts are hotter in bed." "Romance is the core of a good relationship." "Having a few drinks makes better sex." "Only heterosexual relationships are abusive." "If I do what my partner wants, everything will be fine." "It won't happen to me."

What are **your** sexual myths? Where did they originate? It is important to sort them out and acknowledge them for what they are if you want to have clear vision for your journey into sexual happiness.

MYTHS FROM THE LOCKER ROOM, OR "OLD WIVES TALES"

A genuine kiss generates so much heat it destroys germs.

Dr. S. L. Katzoff, San Francisco Inst. of Human Relations

in *You Can't Afford the Luxury of a Negative Thought*

Much of our sexual "education" comes from very unreliable sources. This is true for both genders. Women are bombarded with the advertisers' images of attractiveness that are, at best, unrealistic, and at their worst, lead to anorexia or even suicide because of efforts to conform. According to Parrot, et al. in *"Rape 101"* (Sexual Assault Prevention for College Athletes). "Males are simply not given useful information about sex or sexuality. Instead, men are generally informed by similarly naive peers or pornography." The authors describe many ways in which men are taught to associate sex with violence and with conquest, such as "Scoring (with women) wins points with peers." Another common word is "banging." As you begin to reflect on myths you have heard, do some of these sound familiar?

- "No" really means "Yes."
- "The more togetherness, the better the relationship."
- "As you age, your sexual desire disappears."
- "All you need to know/do is, 'Just Say No.'"
- "You won't get pregnant if you 'do it' standing up."
- "Masturbation will make you crazy."
- "You can get pregnant if you just lie in the same bed."
- "Men can't stop themselves once they are aroused."

What are the sexual myths you were told, and at one time believed, because you trusted the person who told you?

Part of the process of growth and learning is acquiring the ability to distinguish fact from fiction; myths from reality. Honesty in sexual dialogue has not been a strong part of a culture that teaches children that the stork brings babies. We may be glad that we don't have a "FSA" or Federal Sex Administration, but some "truth in telling" might be helpful! Let's look more closely at a few of the more widely accepted myths.

MYTH: "NO REALLY MEANS YES."

There was a time when this was not a myth, so the image is slow to change. Many of us who are older remember as girls being told by peers, if not by parents, that one must appear reluctant when sexually approached, or the boy will think you are "loose." Boys were taught the same message. "Good girls" will pretend they don't want it, but they really do. Fortunately, organizations like Men Against Rape and Athletes for Sexual Responsibility (see bibliography), as well as many women's organizations are working in a powerful way to counter this myth. Women know it is their responsibility to express what they want, and men are learning to trust them.

Myths like this one can create unsurmountable barriers on your path to open and honest relationships if you don't pay attention, and work hard to counter them.

MYTH: "THE BIGGER THE PENIS, THE BETTER THE SEX."

In his excellent, down to earth book for men called *Sexual Solutions* (1980) Michael Castleman discusses "penis size: the universal hang-up." He states:

> *Sex educators try to reassure men that penis size makes no difference in a man's ability to enjoy or give sexual pleasure. They cite the statistics: The average flaccid penis is three inches long. The average erection measures six inches. All erections are about the same size. The smaller the flaccid penis, the greater the growth to erection. The larger the flaccid penis, the less the growth to erection.*

Castleman also refers to a survey done by Bernie Zilbergeld, author of *Male Sexuality,* where a large group of women were asked what they looked for in a lover. The most frequent responses were: tenderness, affection, respect, sensuality, and kindness. Not one woman mentioned penis size. So much for myths of pornography.

MYTH: "THE MORE TOGETHERNESS, THE BETTER THE RELATIONSHIP."

> *Cecelia wanted to be with Tom all the time. After all, she loved him. She questioned Tom's love for her when he wanted to go fishing without her, and didn't seem to want her out in the garage with him when he was working on the car.*

When any two people spend twenty four hours a day together resentments will crop up sooner or later. This is true whether the pair be mother and child, husband and wife, or two brothers. Togetherness is wonderful, but only within limits. Human beings need other human beings, but also some privacy, or alone time. Possessiveness and clinging are signs of insecurity and lack of trust, not mature love.

Usually, one partner's need for space is not exactly the same as the other's. Fortunately, this is usually negotiable. A necessary preliminary step is to assure that the one requiring less space doesn't take his/her partner's need for space, as rejection. The one who needs more space needs to be sensitive to her/his partner's fears, and not be mysterious about where or how the alone time is spent.

MYTH: "AS YOU AGE, YOUR SEXUAL DESIRE DISAPPEARS."

Adelaide shared with the counselor at the senior center that she wanted to go out with men but was tired of the way they all wanted to "jump into bed" on the first date. "But you're over eighty years old!" blurted out the young inexperienced counselor. "Eighty two," replied Adelaide, unperturbed. "The fact is that older men do want sex, and so do women, but women want more emotional involvement, as we always have."

The myth that older people don't have, or want, sex is rapidly disappearing. The reality is that your sex life, once you are older, is determined far more by your life long patterns of sexuality than it is by your age. If you love being sexual when you are younger, you will probably love it as much when you are older. If it was a take it or leave it kind of thing in your 30s, it probably will be the same in your 80s.

Every year in the United States an estimated 56,000 people past the age of 65 marry. The belief that older adults are never promiscuous, and that they do not need sex education, is widespread and false. This is another dangerous myth that can lead to wrecking older lives in an age of AIDS.

THE TRUTH ABOUT AGING AND SEX:

As for women, the changes due to estrogen depletion manifest themselves slowly, generally over a period of many years. The results are:

- Shrinking and thinning of the vaginal wall
- A decrease in the amount of lubrication during sexual arousal
- The uterus becomes smaller, genital tissues and breasts become less firm.

Masters and Johnson found in laboratory studies that older women who continue regular coitus have no difficulty in lubricating and expanding the vagina, even when there is thinning of the vaginal lining. Many older women who have never taken replacement hormones remain sexually active and vigorous to old age. Lubricants are satisfactory if vaginal dryness does occur.

Changes in men's sexuality also take place slowly as they age. The male climacteric begins around age 60 with a slow decline in testosterone (the male sex hormone) but there is not as major a decline in sex hormone production as the aging woman experiences. Decreasing amounts of testosterone may cause older men difficulty in obtaining and maintaining erections, or a decrease in sexual desire. Other age-related changes are:

- Erections are not as full or as hard as in younger men.
- The time to attain a subsequent erection after ejaculation is longer; 12 - 24 hours.
- The ejaculation process slows down.
- It generally takes direct manual stimulation for the penis to become erect.

The degree to which the above changes take place varies from person to person. Even if the changes are extreme, couples find many ways to continue to have mutually satisfying sexual experiences. Literature and other resources are readily available to assist if a couple chooses to avail themselves of them.

MYTH: "JUST SAY NO!"

It is a myth that just saying "no" is an adequate response to the addictions of our times. Whether it's drugs, too much alcohol, intercourse without protection, or harassment. "No" has not stopped rape nor the spread of disease.

It is unfortunate that when we don't know what else to do, there is a tendency to oversimplify, rather than do the hard work of making necessary societal or personal changes. "No" needs to be backed up with conscious awareness of why you want to say no, and awareness of the multiplicity of causes that underlie the issues. Consciousness, conviction, and consistency are important ingredients for success.

In addition, you need skills to apply knowledge with wisdom, good judgement, and tact. Knowledge is power and it provides you with choices. It also helps you feel more in charge of your life. With the hazards that beset you on your course toward loving relationships, "Just say no" comes across not only as inadequate advice, but also as superficial.

COUNTERING ROMANTIC MYTHS:

Probably the most pervasive myths in our world of sex and loving are our "romantic" myths. We are confronted almost daily with the romantic myth that sexual bliss comes from something outside of us. It may be the right perfume, the right car, the right whiskey, or the right person. The more it costs, the more we expect it to solve our problems.

> *We call romantic love ("If only you could find the right person to love, you would live happily ever after") a myth because no other human endeavor has failed so miserably, so often — yet continues to have such "good press."*
>
> John Roger and Peter McWilliams
>
> *DO IT: Let's Get Off Our Buts*

When is romance only a mirage on the horizon, and when is it life and love enhancing? We're regaled with romantic myths. Bridal magazines are not the only ones that paint pictures of wedded bliss that are unrealistic if not misleading to impressionable young women. Men's magazines feed unrealistic myths to young men. George Lucas, talking about movies, tells us that, "If the boy and girl walk off in the sunset hand-in-hand in the last scene, it adds ten million to the box office."

Synonyms of "romantic" according to the dictionary are: *extravagant, exaggerated, wild, improbable,* and *fantastic.* These descriptive words may well apply to the loving relationships you're looking for. But they all refer to qualities that have no staying power. Without stability, trust, interest in your partner's and your own welfare your relationships can leave you, ultimately, with an empty feeling. If romance is the goal at the expense of these more sterling attributes, don't expect to achieve long term loving relationships.

This doesn't mean you have to squelch well-intentioned compliments, or turn into a cynic. It does mean that you try to get to know the other person — who she/he really is — instead of projecting on them what you want or need them to be.

When love is the goal, as opposed to romance, men and women approach relationships as whole persons. You bring your strengths and your weaknesses. You are interested in getting to know someone new, and exploring the potentialities for a new friendship with this other person who also has strengths and weaknesses. When romance is sought to solve problems of loneliness and low self-esteem, the result is rarely love, and the pitfall is more loneliness and lower self-esteem. The love of two whole people with high self-esteem is living at its best.

Why Romance?

Lisa opted for romance as opposed to self-development at several turning points in her life. She dropped out of college to marry. After a divorce she got a job with opportunity for training and promotion, but left it for a clerical job with an oil company so she could follow a new romantic interest overseas. When left stranded in a foreign country, her first thought was to find a man who would rescue her. The one who did was unstable and exploitive.

After returning to the States she continued her pattern of going from one relationship to another with no time in between for reflection or growth. Now, older and wiser, lonely but more insightful, she describes herself as a "relationship junkie" and wishes she'd gotten to know herself instead of devoting all that energy to getting to know, and attract, men. She feels that if she had, she might have established liaisons with men of higher calibre. Instead, as time went on, the ones she did associate with were less and less considerate and responsible.

Lisa is typical of many attractive women in our society who guard what they see as their femininity. They "play dumb," and bad mouth feminists as "too aggressive" (although they believe in equal pay and do not hesitate to benefit from the gains of the feminist movement when it suits them). They stunt their own growth by subordinating their own needs, wills, and wants to those of a man. It's a trade off for romance, or for what they think will afford them security.

Stanton Peele, in *Love and Addiction* writes:

When a person goes to another with the aim of filling a void in him/herself, the relationship quickly becomes the center of his or her life. It offers a solace that contrasts sharply with what s/he finds everywhere else, so s/he returns to it more and more, until s/he needs it to get through each day of an otherwise stressful and unpleasant existence. When a constant exposure to something is necessary in order to make life bearable, an addiction has been brought about, however romantic the trapping.

Since this writing in 1975, hundreds of twelve step programs have been formed to help people deal with this addiction to self-defeating romances. The book, *Women Who Love Too Much* was a run-away best seller.

What are some clues to help you know the difference between mirage and reality? If you review your experiences, you may find that "romance" almost always follows a period of unease or discontent. Real love is more likely to develop when you are feeling strong and confident.

LOVE IS ALSO TAKING OUT THE GARBAGE

Marcia was telling her married friend Sarah about her romantic new lover and how entranced she was with Joe's romantic overtures. She confided that they even took candlelight baths together with music and incense. Sarah was skeptical and said she didn't miss romance – her husband Harry was not inclined toward it – she was too grateful to him for his willingness to scrub the kitchen floor, take care of the baby, and take out the garbage. Marcia was appalled.

A couple of years later when Marcia was left home to care for her newborn while Joe was out romancing other women, Sarah was too kind to say, "I told you so." But they both agreed that willingness to take out the garbage was preferable to receiving roses, and candlelight bathing; the important element being a solid foundation of authentic love.

It's wise to give some thought to what's important to you in a relationship. For example, Enid, when in romantic situations, tended to forget that a positive and understanding attitude toward her son by a previous marriage was more important to her than frequent trips to Atlantic City to gamble. Her mother, married for forty five years, focused on whether her husband held the door for her when she got in and out of the car, instead of trying to refer him to Gamblers' Anonymous, a referral that could have saved their marriage.

Academy Award winning actress Shirley Jones, and her husband, Marty Ingels, described the meaning of love in "Modern Maturity Magazine" (November-December, 1995). While inclined toward the romantic, and touting its value, Shirley also claims that real love is "selfless, sacrificial and unconditional." Marty, who claims to be more pragmatic, says:

> *Somebody has to stay sober during Happy Hour, and sometimes that means taking a good hard look at the happy stuff we're swallowing to make sure it's good brew and not a one-night, full-mooned ticket to disappointment and despair. That means...testing that new love (in the worst of times), weighing that new love (with the passing of time), and, yes, analyzing that new love in the unforgiving glare of morning light. And, if it passes all those tests, then it will sparkle and bubble so much brighter in that Saturday-night goblet, for it will have proved itself to be not only sweet, but dependable; not only here, but anywhere, not only tonight, but tomorrow night.*

From the dialogue of these two happily married (for 21 years) celebrities, it is clear that a stable relationship can have its fair share of romance without sacrificing good judgment.

Gloria Steinem, well known writer and feminist suggests in her book, *Revolution From Within,*[1] "The internal wholeness that allows one to love both one's self and another, freely and joyously, is hard to find anywhere. On the other hand, the personal wreckage caused by romantic obsession is a feature of our everyday landscape." When asked whether high self-esteem will cause romance to wither away, Steinem replied,

> *Yes - but only in its current form. After all, romance is one additional very important thing: the most intense form of curiosity. If we weren't so needy, so full of illusions about a magic rescue, so hooked on trying to own someone - in other words, if the conscious goal of romance were stretching our understanding of ourselves and others... romance could be a deep, intimate, sensual, empathetic way of learning; of seeing through someone else's eyes, absorbing another culture or way of life from the inside, stretching our boundaries, and bringing into ourselves a wider view of the world.*

So our task is not to deny romance, but to distinguish it from romantic illusions based on incompleteness, excessive neediness. and other forms of insecurity.

GETTING CLEAR ABOUT YOUR MYTHS AND REALITY:

Whether your personal sexual myths have to do with romance, with finding that perfect partner, or other fantasies, the challenge is to sort them out. What is real for you, and what is based on illusion? Be as clear as you can about what you really want instead of what you think you ought to want. Why waste time pursuing a myth? There is an exciting reality that is much more achievable and long lasting. Too often self-esteem gets damaged because someone is unsuccessful in fulfilling a dream. Dreams or goals based on reality have a much greater chance of success.

So filter out the myths that your family or your culture have taught you. This is a vital step in planning for your long term sexual happiness.

1 Steinem, Gloria, *Revolution From Within: A Book of Self-Esteem,* Little Brown & Co., New York, NY 10020, 1992

TO DO LIST

1. Think of people you know well, or that you have been in a relationship with in the past. Can you identify some myths that you feel they were using to guide their behavior?

2. Select a sexual myth that you used to believe, but now know to be false. What helped you to figure out the reality?

3. Recall some sexual situations you were in where you were not happy about the way you handled yourself. Try to identify one or more sexual myths that influenced you to behave in the way that you did. ("Men prefer women who act helpless" or "women like to be pressured.")

4. Check the first draft of your sexual self-contract to see if you included any myths as goals or conditions. If so, re-evaluate that choice and consider a more realistic one.

CHAPTER 5

BE THE CAPTAIN OF YOUR SHIP

When one is a stranger to oneself, then one is estranged from others, too. If one is out of touch with oneself, then one cannot touch others.

Anne Morrow Lindbergh, *Gift from the Sea, 1955*

If your goal is to have a relationship that is a loving, sharing partnership, yet it isn't happening, you may be making a common mistake. If you are already in a relationship that isn't meeting your expectations, you may be looking to the other person for the desired changes, rather than focusing on your own options for action. If so, you know that it is difficult, if not impossible, to change someone else. Putting your energy into yourself will be much more effective and less frustrating. You can learn how to act instead of react, and how to model the changes you seek. You can't really love someone else until you've learned to love yourself. Trying to achieve love from the outside without first generating it from the inside doesn't work. Don't let someone else steer your ship.

WHERE DID YOUR SEXUAL ATTITUDES COME FROM?

Parents are role models of sexual interaction and their behavior has more of an impact than anything they might say.

Claudette asked her mother where babies come from and her mother told her she was too young to understand, and shouldn't be thinking about such things at her age. Claudette made it her business to find out from her friends at school. The information she received was so distorted that she was totally unprepared to take care of herself. She was raped by a date, and didn't have anyone to confide in. She felt stupid, guilty, and alone.

Our self-image as attractive or not, bright or stupid, fun or dull, is usually based on family attitudes, the roles we were assigned as children in the family constellation.

The statistics on family violence show that men and women batterers almost always come from homes where violence was used as a way to settle disputes. By the same token, children brought up in homes where sexuality is a natural, healthy part of life, a way that partners express their love for each other, are apt to have fewer hang-ups.

Amanda was molested by her father on and off from the time that she was ten until she was fifteen and ran away from home. Her mother didn't believe her, and made her feel guilty for "lying." Amanda's reaction to sex was confusion, fear, guilt, shock, and anger.

It isn't difficult to understand why Amanda was incapable of relating in an open, trusting way until she had benefitted from long term therapy. Tragically, various versions of these scenarios are common. If your sexual hang-ups are the result of severe childhood sexual trauma, it is advisable to get counseling to deal with post traumatic reactions and sort out your feelings.

For each person, the process of getting to know the sexual side of themselves will be different. You are the judge of the approach that is best for you. Because careful sexual self-examination can be intense, many experts recommend that you choose to abstain from sex for a period of time while you think through your goals and get to know yourself. If you choose to do this, you may be accused of being "unrealistic," "prudish," or "uptight." Don't let that deter you. Start with looking at yourself, and working on your self-esteem and your self-care skills. You have a right to make decisions about your own body.

Then again, abstention may not work for you now. Maybe you feel it would be damaging to a relationship you are already in, or you are trying to build. This choice does not need a majority vote or a consensus. It is yours alone. If you don't choose abstention, you may have more difficulty in becoming clear about who you are sexually, but you can continue working on changing your sexual life and intimacy patterns to meet your goals.

DO YOU LOVE YOURSELF?

When you think of loving yourself, you may think of people you know who are self-serving or always bragging about themselves. Your thoughts may be "I don't want to be like that!" Good, because that is not self-love. That is covering for insecurities, fear or self-hate. Truly loving yourself includes accepting the reality of who you are; accepting what you have done and not done. You don't have to prove yourself to anyone. You don't try to fit yourself into someone else's idea of who you ought to be. By accepting yourself, and being true to the best that is you, you are able to understand and honor others for who they are. You can be clear about the person with whom you wish to share your sexual self.

Ron and Mary Hulnick (University of Santa Monica, CA) offer a guide to nurturing, honoring, and accepting yourself:

"Because I am the only person I will have a relationship with all of my life, I choose:"

- To love myself the way I am now
- To always acknowledge that I am enough just the way I am
- To love, honor and cherish myself
- To be my own best friend
- To be the person I would like to spend the rest of my life with
- To always take care of myself so that I can take care of others
- To always grow, develop and share my love and life

One way to know if you love yourself is to watch the messages you tell yourself. Pay attention to your "self-talk." Do you put yourself down when you make a mistake? Do you say to yourself, "What an idiot. I knew better than to do that." Instead, are you able to say, "I don't feel good about what I did, so what can I learn from that choice so I'll feel better next time?" Watch for "I can't," "I always," and "I never." When you use these all-or-nothing words, they are seldom correct. You are probably reacting more to your worst fears about yourself than to your reality.

Self-talk may be perpetuating negative messages that you received about yourself when you were younger from your parents and other family members. If you catch yourself, stop and do two things. First, praise yourself for recognizing the pattern and catching yourself doing it. Second, rephrase your thought so that it is more positive and precise based on your current reality. "I always mess up" can become "I notice that my work is not as accurate when I am worrying about my relationship. I will talk to my partner tonight so I can put that aside now and concentrate on work."

What are your sexual self put-downs? Be aware if you tell yourself you're unattractive, and remind yourself that not everyone is handsome or beautiful, but that every man and woman has attractive traits that can be developed.

Do you tell yourself that you're stupid? Better to acknowledge that you've made a mistake, goofed, or are not informed than brand yourself with a totally negative evaluation. And if you find yourself calling yourself names, stop it. Counter all such negative self-talk and replace it with positive strokes.

Another clue to know if your personal self-critic is overactive is to notice how often you apologize for something over which you had little or no control. You invite someone for dinner, and when they arrive in the rain you say, "I'm sorry it is such a wet night." Or how about, "I'm sorry I'm on my period," or "I'm sorry I don't have a fancier car to take you in." Perhaps the car is really a good choice, given your financial priorities. Watch for times when you apologize. Ask yourself if the responsibility or power for change rests with you or with someone else. Often it is elsewhere.

Do you find that you frequently apologize for decisions you've made? Do you apologize when you ask for specific sexual responses, or refuse them? Was there really any fault involved? Or are you apologizing because you know the other person wanted a different result, even though you believe you made the best choice? Sometimes an attempt to please others too much can have damaging consequences to your own self-esteem and your personal effectiveness. Even though it may seem to please the other person at the time, your apology may really be an insult.

You are saying you don't have enough confidence in that person or in your relationship to express your feelings.

Loving yourself is being able to look at yourself honestly and to accept what you see. It is to feel confident that it's O.K. to make the changes you would like, without self-deprecation or apology.

YOUR SEXUAL SELF-IMAGE

To what extent does your body-image agree with the reality of your flesh-and-blood body? The anorexic, no matter how emaciated, sees herself as fat. When a person chooses losers as partners, it could reflect his/her own level of self-esteem. Studies report that self-assessments of women differ more from reality than the self-assessments of men. Such variations contribute to low self-esteem.

Inaccurate body or sex self-images are tenacious. Every compliment is discounted, and any bit of negative feed-back is perceived as confirmation of the person's paltry self-perception. These self-perceptions fluctuate with changes in environments and experiences, but "core," or "global" self-esteem, as it is called, remains fairly stable.

Your sexual self-image underpins your level of self-esteem. If it is low, your more apt to be self-defeating. In a survey of 400 U.S. psychiatrists published by *Medical Aspects of Human Sexuality*, the majority reported that both women and men with low self-esteem were more likely to be promiscuous, to have difficulty finding fulfillment in sexual relationships, and to be **less** likely to fall **deeply** in love.

Gloria Steinem writes that with low self-esteem, men and women grow more polarized and have more suppressed parts of themselves to project on to others. "...with low self-esteem, both males and females are likely to seek refuge and approval in exaggerated versions of their gender roles, thus to become even less complete as they grow up. Inflexibility, dogmatism, competitiveness, aggression, distance from any female quality or person, homophobia, even cruelty and violence, become the classic gender masks of low self-esteem in men. Submissiveness, dependency, need for male approval, fear of conflict, self-blame, and inability to express anger are classic gender masks of low self-esteem in women."

Do You Love Your Sexual Self?

You can have high self-esteem in many areas of your life, and still be disabled by hidden or elusive sexual attitudes.

Marty was intelligent, witty, had a good job, and was fun to be with. He had many women friends. However, as soon as one of them started to act romantically interested, he would shy away. He felt his body was too skinny, and he was afraid for a woman to see it. Because of his fears, he didn't dare get too close to intimacy, even though it was what he really wanted.

Marty was accepting a sexual myth that being big and muscular was a pre-requisite to attracting a loving partner. By not accepting his body he denied himself the opportunity to enter into a loving relationship. He also deprived others of enjoying him. It is important to let others choose what attracts them. Don't pre-judge! It's worth risking a few rejections to find a person who adores you as you are.

Are you comfortable with your professional, parenting, or social self, but not with yourself in intimate relationships? Have you lost a good, loving relationship, and don't trust yourself to develop a new one?

An important first step toward loving your sexual self is to know who you really are sexually. How do others see you? What are your sexual values and ethics? Are you sometimes baffled by your own sexual feelings or behaviors? It is difficult to love a part of you that you don't understand, or that doesn't behave according to your standards. Who you are sexually is a complex mixture of genetics, hormones, learned values, past experiences and future goals and dreams. The better you know this part of you, the more you are able to influence your sexual self in the direction you desire.

DO YOU KNOW WHAT DRIVES YOU SEXUALLY?

There may me times when you are not aware of what drives you sexually. Do you find yourself attracted to a person who has very little in common with you, and yet not interested in someone who, by all reasonable assessments, would be a better partner?

Since her divorce, friends had arranged for several blind dates for Sheila with kind and decent men. But Sheila was bored and frustrated. She found herself seeking out men who were very different from herself. After many wild weekends, she realized that a long term relationship with a new, exciting person would never work. Then she would feel more alone, as if there was no hope for her ever finding the relationship she really wanted. She began to isolate herself.

The challenge of knowing your sexual self is to access what you know in your depths so you can view it with clarity and have more control over it. Something buried deep under the ocean of your experiences may be out of sight, but it is having an impact on what happens on the surface.

One way to examine yourself and your sexuality is to find a quiet time alone and dialogue with yourself. You might ask, "When do I feel good about myself?" "What would I most like to change about how I act in intimate situations?" "What aspect of my sexual self do I value the most?" You might be surprised at what a good conversationalist you can be with yourself.

All of us know more than we think we know. At any given time, your conscious, thinking mind can focus only on a very small percent of what your inner self knows. Yet much of your behavior is guided (or controlled) by this inner information. When an idea or a feeling seems to come to you out of the blue, it can be that inner information coming to the surface. You may call it a gut feeling, or intuition. If it's a positive idea or feeling you might say "Just a good guess," or "I got lucky." If it's negative, you might say, "I'm scared," or "Count me out." Learning to know the source of these impulses, and to understand them consciously is a big step in taking charge of your sexual self. Knowledge of what drives you from the inside is one kind of power.

People learn and remember on many different levels. The new biology and physics paradigms tell us that every cell has memory. This gives us information about disease and health, in the mind-body connections. Massage can trigger what is called body memories. Strong feelings suddenly burst forth when pressure is put on a part of the body, with no conscious thought as to where the emotions come from.

Pam is playing soccer for her college team. Another player trips, and falls hard against Karen's right thigh, knocking her down. She bursts into hysterical tears. It is several minutes before she can get herself under control. Generally she takes hits and falls with no problem. She can't understand why she reacted so strongly. Later, with the help of a therapist, she is able to recall a painful childhood memory where being hit in the same place with a ball was tied to painful rejection by her "first love." This release helped heal Pam's childhood wound, and made it possible for her present boyfriend to stroke her thigh without her jerking away; a reaction she hadn't understood before.

Sometimes your "gut responses" are on target and helpful. Other times they may get you into trouble. Why? Many responses that come from other than a conscious thought, come from old learned patterns that worked for you in a similar situation in the past, but may not be appropriate in the present.

Sue, recently divorced, has just begun to date. She is at a party. She has one drink. Before the party, she had planned to stop at one. While Sue is deeply engaged in an interesting conversation, the waitress arrives, asking "one more round?" The person Sue is speaking with gives an enthusiastic "You bet!" and all the others near concur. Sue feels a sense of urgency to respond, but feels immobilized. She says nothing. This sense of urgency is a good key to unlocking her capacity to choose. If her personal "computer" perceives that there is no time to think through a new response, it looks for a similar situation in the past, and grabs a response that worked before. Probably one from her teen years. It's not the one she truly wants. It's her old pattern; to say nothing.

Habitual responses, long ingrained and unexamined in the present, are hard to change.

Myrtle always did exactly what the Doctor said. She was a model of compliance, and submissive to the point that she offered little information and didn't ask questions. It took some serious symptoms and much pressure, from her daughter, for her to agree to share more with her Doctor and Pharmacist, ask questions, and take more responsibility for collaborating with them in managing her own health care. A sexually transmitted disease was then treated before it got out of control and did serious damage to her physically.

There are many reasons to access your inner information. You can take more control over your own life, choices, and behavior. You will raise your level of inner joy and inner peace. Self-esteem and self-confidence both go up dramatically. Insight alone is not enough to change your behavior, but it's a sound basis on which to build a new self-image and new patterns of reaction. You can then act instead of react.

CLARIFYING PERSONAL SEXUAL CONFUSIONS:

Do you get turned on when you least expect it? Do you think something will be wonderful, and then find that it's a turn-off? This kind of confusion about your own sexual responses or feelings is common. Fortunately, the answers are within you, and with a little work, you can find some of them.

First, list what you remember as being sexually exciting or as having given you joy in the past. Recall those high moments you treasure. Be as specific as you can about time, place, color, smells, people. Now, make another list of what you imagine might excite you if you had the opportunity to experience it. List the behaviors or experiences that, in your fantasy or imagination, you want to experience, but so far have not.

Set these lists aside. Take a break. Now, do the same for what has turned you off or brought you down. List the gestures, words, places, smells, and experiences that have turned you off, sexually. Focus on the part that was the most bothersome to you, even if you don't think it would have seemed that way to others. Now, add experiences that you believe would turn you off if you did experience them.

Do your two lists contain some of the same things? What was the difference? Something that brings joy at one time, might not at others. What are the differences? Clearly, the difference lies within you, not the action. What does it mean to you? Are you influenced by what you believe to be the intention of the other person? By your personal goals in the moment? By past similar experiences?

Pam's positive list included when her date stroked her hair on graduation night, as they walked on a deserted golf course in the moonlight. Her negative list included when her uncle followed her into the bathroom and stroked her hair while she was combing it. The stroking wasn't the issue. Her feeling about the person's intention, and the person, made all the difference.

What does this say about how Pam will feel when her lover strokes her hair? She has both the negative and the positive emotion tied to it. By understanding this, she can talk to her partner and get help in clearing the negative image. One way is for a partner to ask permission. At first, she may want to be asked with words. Later a look or gesture may suffice, and eventually, permission will be generalized, so that they both know there is no need to ask. By taking charge of what happens to her body, and having that accepted, trust is built.

DEEPENING YOUR SEXUAL SELF AWARENESS:

Write the beginnings of each of these sentences, and add some of your own. Complete the sentences 10 times each, putting down whatever comes to your head, without evaluation or editing:

I feel sexy when _____

I like it when my sexual partner _____

I don't like it when my sexual partner_____

I feel good about my choices when I_____

I wish that I had not _____

I wish that I would _____._____

Sue's responses to the first question looked like this:

- I feel sexy when I wear dark make up.

- I feel sexy when someone whistles at me.

- I feel sexy when I wear silky clothes.
- I feel sexy when I ride in a red car.
- I feel sexy when I sip cappuccino in a cafe.
- I feel sexy when someone tells me I look good.
- I feel sexy when I smell Old Spice.
- I feel sexy when I dangle my feet in a stream or pool.
- I feel sexy when I wear green.
- I feel sexy when I dance all by myself.

As she examined her list, she realized that most of the first ones were related to cultural expectations or advertising. Later ones were more personal, and related to specific experiences in her life. These helped her recall the underlying reasons for her feelings.

Usually the first 4 or 5 answers are from your most conscious thoughts, and may even include some "shoulds," or what you believe are the "right" answers. As you get to the 7th answer or later, you're more apt to tap into inner reasons. You will know it when you do. Examine these, and dialogue with yourself about the source of these answers. The insight may amaze you.

How do you come across to others? Short of having very honest friends that you can ask, or very honest non-friends that blurt out truths, knowing how you are seen by others can be difficult!

You could start by looking in the mirror. One problem here is that most of us have our "look-in-the-mirror" look. We square our shoulders, smile, or in some other way work to create what we hope to see. A more effective use of the mirror for self understanding is to sit in front of it getting as full a view as possible. Imagine yourself in different situations looking at different people you know, "freeze" your expression, then glance in the mirror and note your expression. This can be shocking.

Another tool for taking an honest look at how others see you is to ask five same sex friends and five different sex friends, each without the other's knowledge, to tell you five words that they would use to describe you. This in itself can be very enlightening. If you want to go into greater depth, you might ask them more probing questions, such as what they see as:

- Your most attractive physical feature
- Your most problematic physical trait
- Your most attractive personality quality
- A personality quality that might be improved

You can choose your own questions based on your areas of special interest. After each time, write them down. Memories can play tricks. After you get all 10 (or more if you're ambitious), compare and look for similarities and patterns. If only one person makes a comment, it probably says more about that person than it does about you. (Be careful here! Often when you feel vulnerable, you look for the worst and dwell on it. You get 5 A's and focus on the one B.) Learning not to claim what does not belong to you is another valuable skill. It keeps you from being so vulnerable to others hurting you, and less likely to try to solve your pain by hurting others.

If several people say the same thing about you, their comments are worth considering. It may be something you already know about yourself, but don't like to face, or it may be something that's a surprise to you. If you would find it too uncomfortable to ask directly, or feel your friends would have difficulty coming up with descriptive words, you can make up a comment sheet, using words that you wonder about in relationship to yourself, and put it out as a personal growth survey. Offer them a copy to use in developing their own survey. You could use the "PERSONAL GROWTH SURVEY" below, but your personalized one might give you better information. This might be a questionnaire that you would like to ask yourself, as if you were your own best friend.

You are always learning. You know more about yourself now than you did yesterday. The challenge is to let go of old patterns and integrate new information into your behavior.

PERSONAL GROWTH SURVEY

- If you were to describe me (or insert your name), using only five carefully chosen descriptive words, what words would you choose?

_____

_____

_____

_____

_____

- In your opinion, what is my most attractive physical feature?

- If you had to suggest one thing for me to do, that I could do, to improve the way I present myself physically, what would you suggest?

- What is there about my personality that you find most attractive or pleasant?

- If you had to suggest one thing for me to do to enhance my personality or how I relate to others, what would you suggest?

TO DO LIST

- List in your draft contract one or more qualities that you especially like about yourself that you want to preserve.

- List at least one trait that you want to change.

- Check your self-contract to be sure your guidelines for your future reflect your present day beliefs and desires and not old, ingrained patterns or imperatives from your past.

CHAPTER 6

MESSAGES: SENDING AND RECEIVING

Misunderstandings often cause confusion and embarrassment, especially in the area of sexual communication. Misread signals can lead to detours on your way to achieving your goal of loving relationships. When you misinterpret another's conversation as having romantic overtones, and you're mistaken, it can be devastating.

EMBARRASSING MOMENTS

Embarrassing moments can result from mixed or misunderstood sexual signals and be ripples on the surface of your self-esteem, or they can grow into tidal waves that unnerve you. If sexual signals are not clear, honest, and direct, havoc can result. For example:

Gail had an experience with a younger man that she found humiliating. He offered her brownies, and she, unaware that they were laced with marijuana, ate several. Then he seduced her.

Should she attribute this to a generation gap? She wondered if it would be rude to ask a date if he'd spiked the punch, added marijuana to food, or otherwise tricked her. Yes, it's O.K. to ask! If you have allergies, wouldn't you ask the hostess if the allergen was in the food? If a date takes offense at a direct question of this nature, do you think he/she would be capable of establishing a positive relationship?

Molly was mortified when, after responding to Dick's attentions and getting romantically excited, she realized that he was really interested in her 18 year old daughter. It forced her to face that she is now part of the "older generation."

Embarrassment must be viewed as a wavelet, not an unsurmountable obstacle. A sense of humor is probably the greatest tool for surmounting it.

Novelist Cera McFadden is a perfect example. In an article in "New Choices" (March 1995), titled, *Singles Dating; Finding Happiness in the Minefield,*[1] she relates that after being widowed she began to go out on dates. "Dating made me feel young again — fifteen, to be precise, and a panicky mess." Her skin broke out. "Life became an endless bad-hair day...even the word 'dating' made me self-conscious....inside the adult woman was a teenager desperate for her date's approval and certain that she'd commit some gaffe — a self-fulfilling prophecy." Is it comforting to know that otherwise sensible people who are deprived of a partner by death or divorce, stripped of the comforts of coupledom, are insecure about dating again regardless of their age?

Often unattached older women feel like leftovers at a banquet unless they develop healthy self-images and enjoy their own company. It helps if they've learned over the years to value and nurture the friendship of other women. It takes courage to venture beyond your comfort zone, out into the world of dating. As psychotherapist Harville Hendrix put it in his book, *Keeping the Love You Find: A Guide for Singles* (Pocket Books), "We're people brought up by the old rules but playing by the new." Embarrassment is based, of course, on a fear of what people will think of you.

Even Letitia Baldrige of "Good Manners" gets queries on the subject. A reader wrote:

Q.: *I look a lot younger than my 55 years. Two months ago I met a younger man while on vacation in Hawaii. We got along very well and he is coming to visit me shortly. The problem is, he has no idea how old I really am, and I'm becoming increasingly nervous about being seen with him here in my community for fear that my friends will start gossiping behind my back. Should I just cancel his planned visit?*

Ms. Baldrige's sensible reply can be generalized to answer similar challenges regarding embarrassment or fear of "what people will say":

A.: *Don't cancel your new friend's trip to visit you. Have a good time with him, and if you feel your friends are talking about him behind your back, they're not your real friends. In fact, they are probably just jealous.*

It helps to realize that you are not alone. No one ever died of embarrassment (though, as McFadden says, there's always a first time!).

Even Miss Manners gets "into the act," this act meaning the confusion about getting and giving sexual signals. One of her readers wrote:

I'm currently single, attractive and available. However, I've been trying for one year to catch this perfect man. We work in the same place of business, so I see him often, but he's a hard catch. I've given him many signs that I'm interested, and he also has shown some interest, yet nothing has happened. His schedule is very busy. I'm wondering if this man is just playing games, really interested, or gay. I've heard he was married. But my concern is how to catch him. I want him! Do I give up? Or go for it? Do I openly confront him?

Miss Manners, with her usual aplomb, replied:

Gentle Reader: And demand to know why he has behaved pleasantly to a co-worker, if he doesn't mean her to catch him? Or explain that while being gay might be an acceptable excuse from having a romance with you, being married isn't?

Miss Manners wouldn't put it past you. She is afraid, however, that the most you can properly do is to propose to the gentleman that you get together outside of work. If he says he is too busy, you are required to accept this answer as final — gracefully and cheerfully so as not to disturb the working relationship.

There are two warnings Miss Manners should give you:

1. *Being busy is etiquette's euphemism to allow people to show lack of romantic interest without resorting to such unpleasantries as 'Not if you were the last person left on earth.' It is a safe assumption that anyone truly eager to begin a romance finds time for it, in spite of all other demands.*

2. *Romantically pursuing colleagues who do not respond to restrained hints is not only rude - now, it's illegal.*

SEXUAL HARASSMENT

The persistent sending of unwanted sexual messages goes beyond embarrassment and misunderstanding. It is a form of emotional abuse now known as "sexual harassment." As a legal term, it refers to work or school. The Equal Employment Opportunity Commission (EEOC) defines sexual harassment as "unwelcome sexual or gender-based behavior that has the purpose or effect of adversely affecting a person's working or learning environment." Generally there's an imbalance of power, where a professor offers higher grades for sexual favors, or a boss or supervisor implies that sexual cooperation will lead to company advancement.

When you get questions about your sexual behavior, demeaning comments about your gender, sexually oriented jokes, or conversations full of innuendoes or double meanings, you are being harassed. Older people are not immune. There are many jokes about "dirty old men," and greeting cards often demean older adults' sexual interest or ability. These harassing messages can wear away at your sense of sexual safety and self-esteem.

Sexual harassment is quite common. Surveys show that it has been experienced by twenty to thirty percent of college women, fifty to seventy percent of employed women, and ten to fifteen percent of men in college and the workplace. It can happen to anyone. It can lead to people dropping out of school or changing majors, leaving jobs, and having major emotional traumas.

Ignoring these unwanted sexual signals is often not enough to stop them. Sometimes it is so serious that you need to take legal action, like a restraining order. However, sending good, clear messages back is often effective. Sometimes non-verbal messages, like moving away, a look of dislike or disgust, or gesturing the person to go away, will work. If not, taking the person aside, and saying something like, "I have the impression you are sending me sexual messages. If you are, you need to know that I am not interested in that kind of a relationship with you, so please stop, and we can continue to have a decent working relationship." If this doesn't work, go to your superior so the harassment can be stopped as soon as possible.

As in other situations, awareness is a good first step to safety. The harasser may not be as you'd hoped, or the attitude of workers or students may disappoint you, but acceptance of the reality, with knowledge and planning, can help you take the most appropriate action to keep yourself safely on your way to cultivating more positive relationships.

QUESTIONS YOU'RE AFRAID TO ASK

The mixed messages — scenes of recreational, sado-masochistic, violent, and explicit sex nightly on T.V. while churches are still preaching pre-marital abstinence — make formulating one's own ethics and rearing children confusing and problematic.

New knowledge has brought with it new problems that you can perceive as so frightening that you go to one extreme or the other. That is, withdraw from new liaisons, or say to yourself that you're not going to live the life of a monk, and become promiscuous. How do you respond to today's changing sexual challenges on a personal level in a way that moves you along your charted course toward sexual health?

Cheryl wants to date, and become sexually active but she does not know how to deal with her fear of pregnancy. She wants to know how to ask a date if he has protection with him, but is too embarrassed to ask. In her women's support group, one person who tended to be an aggressive comedian role-played it, "Your place or mine? Your condom or my diaphragm?" Everyone laughed and the consensus was that humor sometimes works, but Cheryl didn't feel comfortable with that approach.

What would you do if you were in Cheryl's situation? Or how would you advise her?

Other suggestions from the group ranged from abstinence, to bringing up the subject obliquely by initiating a discussion of abortion rights. Because of the support of the group, Cheryl gave herself permission to take more time than she'd planned. She felt less scared and less desperate. In a few weeks she reported with much self-satisfaction that she and her date were getting more and more comfortable with each other. In fact, when the subject did come up—someone they both knew was dropping out of college due to pregnancy—discussing birth control seemed the most natural thing in the world. They were not in a hurry, but she felt good about the way they were building trust in each other.

Humor, assertiveness, an oblique approach to a charged subject, or direct questions are all acceptable options. The guidelines are: Don't put your partner down either deliberately or inadvertently. Don't put yourself down, either. And don't try to get your way through manipulation.

Another example of someone needing to ask awkward questions:

Christopher faced going out on a date with another divorced person and, from conversation and reputation, they knew they had both "been around." How to find out if she'd been tested for HIV? "If I come right out with it it could ruin what could be a very decent relationship. Is it up to me or up to her? If I wait too long I'll be taking a life-threatening risk. What do I do?"

What would you do? How would you advise Christopher?

Some start with general dialogue: "What do you think of the feminist movement? Do you think women and men can fully understand each other or have a relationship in which they can talk about anything?" Perhaps for Christopher, "Things are so different, and even dangerous now. I've even been tested for AIDS. If anyone had told me five years ago that that would be a concern of mine I would have been shocked. Have you been tested?"

Another oblique lead-in can be to question whether your date works in a place where AIDS testing is required. But at a certain point it's best to be direct. "Would you be willing to be tested for AIDS?" As simple as that. If that freaks him/her out too much, maybe he or she is not for you.

Along with communicating fear of an unwanted pregnancy, and sexually transmitted diseases, there's the challenge of responding to the signal that your date is drunk. Being trapped in a car with a drunken driver is another hazard. This, too, is a predicament where assertive skills are a must. A passive approach is to get in the car, let him/her drive, and risk lives. To get into an aggressive confrontation could be dangerous. This situation requires confidence and skills in assertiveness. It's another case where having a self-contract, one that contains your resolve to not drink and drive or ride with drunken drivers, can be empowering. It's wise to get help, a taxi, or another ride in such circumstances.

As more people live alone and date many years before marrying, there's a greater need for clarifying expectations. This is true not only to survive embarrassing moments, but also to make wise decisions in life-threatening situations.

WHEN YOU'RE SCARED OF REJECTION

No one likes to be rejected. Suppose that the message you're receiving is that you're being dumped. An effective strategy is to practice your assertive skills and apply them, where possible, with humor. For example, Phoebe was crazy about Max. When he went to Mexico on business, he didn't tell her in advance. She was crushed. But when she was asked, "How's Max?" she managed to reply, "Oh, he went to Mexico to forget me!"

Andrea's response, in similar circumstances, was, "I fired him." After a man that McFadden liked dropped out of her life – they'd met a few times for coffee – by reflex, she wondered what she'd done wrong. "Then," she said, "I had a bout of mental health. Oh well, I thought, his loss."

Joel was so insecure that when he received mild criticism, he blurted out, "I don't need this nagging, I'm out of here." In this way he ended potentially positive relationships prematurely out of his fear of rejection.

This kind of fear is a bugaboo, but it can be countered. One way to lower your anxiety level and increase your enjoyment is to look at dating as building friendships and expanding your social and support network; not as a courtship ritual only. This doesn't mean that you shouldn't give yourself time to grieve your losses and recover from rejections. It means that it helps to keep your perspective. Whether you see your significant others like streetcars, (in the old maxim, another will be coming along any moment), or as fish (there are plenty in the sea), or whatever metaphor, there's a basis for hope for future satisfying connections. Hope and humor can go a long way in surviving dating games.

LISTENING FOR SEXUAL MESSAGES

With intimate, sexual relationships, your listening skills are probably even more important than your ability to verbalize well. Some of the values of good listening are:

- **Listening can build relationships.** You will be valued and appreciated for letting the other person talk and for listening attentively to his/her thoughts and feelings.

- **Listening can reduce tension.** It gives others a chance to get problems or views off their chests and may help to clear the air of tension and hostility.

- **Listening can be informative.** You can learn about various subjects, or a different point of view, but when it comes to sexual communication, the point is that you can learn a lot about your partner or potential partner.

- **Listening may solve a problem** for the other person. Just giving a person a chance to talk through a problem to you may give needed clarification.

- **Listening leads to better cooperation** because when people feel listened to, they are more able to listen, and the other person is more receptive to seeing your point of view.

- **Listening can prevent problems.** Too often when you talk before you listen you make comments you regret.

- **Listening can give you confidence.** With careful listening you will be more confident that your understanding of the person and/or topic is accurate, and what you say in response will be relevant.

- **Listening gives you time to think.** The average speaking rate is about 125 words per minute and the average listening capacity is about 400-600 words per minute. Thus, as listener, you have about 75 percent of your time available for organizing what you hear, tuning-in to nonverbals, and gaining understanding of the larger picture — bringing your contract to mind and to bear.

When you're listening effectively, you are not thinking about what you will say next. You are focused on figuring out how the other person is thinking and feeling. Your responses may take a moment, but they will be more on target. If both of you listen well, the chance of your having a good relationship, or agreeing that it won't work, are enhanced.

NONVERBAL SEXUAL MESSAGES

Another source of conflicting sexual expectations comes from inaccurate "reading" of nonverbal language. Body language varies in different cultures; even in different families or individuals. Downcast eyes can be respect or avoidance. Crossed legs can be comfortable, or feeling closed and shut off. Certain gestures may have a positive meaning in one culture and negative in another. Past president Nixon learned this when he gave what we consider the peace sign of two fingers in a "V" at a public gathering in a country where the "V" had the same meaning as holding up one middle finger has in our culture. One family may have a signal that means thank you, while in another family the same signal might mean "I'm ignoring what you want and will do what I want." This is why you must "read" all body language with a question mark, and find ways to affirm or correct your impressions before acting on them.

If you are around someone for a while, you can discover habitual gestures. Then you will notice when there is a change. A change in habitual gestures and other body movements can indicate strong internal emotions. Here are some nonverbal clues that it's time to pay close attention.

- When words don't fit the gesture:

  Have you ever seen someone exclaim, "Oh, I'd love to!" as they shake their head no? Or when you say you are shy, and someone responds, "I am really shy, too" as they move into your personal space? The basic rule is believe the body more than the words. Words are easier to fake.

- Watch for motions that move up, vs. move down:

  When a person wants to help or uplift you, gestures are more apt to be open, expansive, and move upwards. A wave of the arm up and out while some one says, "Let me show you" feels like they want to empower you. Up and in can be a desire to join with you. When someone says, "Let me show you," and gestures by waving the arm down (a gesture some use for "It was nothing"), it is more apt to be that they are minimizing you, or feeling that you are stupid and need them. This is more a "You poor person, where would you be without me?" gesture.

- Excessive movement:

Some people are much more physically active than others. Watch for individual patterns of behavior so you can distinguish between them and flirting, seductive gestures, significant postures, fondling of hair and other parts of the body, etc.

Sexually charged messages can be sent by women or men by continually running their hands through their hair, or licking their lips as they eat with exaggerated sensual gusto. Stroking arms, neck, and shoulders can be provocative, and women's clothing can make many sexual statements. Ultra short mini-skirts, tight sweaters, and all sorts of decolletage are often sexual signals.

Eyes communicate, too. For example, eyes that won't meet yours, but cruise your body. Body language communicates whether it's much fondling on a first date, standing or sitting close with maximum body contact, or "pushing" into your space.

Whether you're sending or receiving messages, pay attention to body language, your own and others'. This will help increase the depth and quality of your relationships.

TEST YOUR SKILL AT SENDING NON-VERBAL SIGNALS

1. Make a list of feelings that are important in your life. Use the following list for suggestions. Every age group, culture, class and location has different words that are used more commonly. Use words that are familiar to you.

2. Choose a partner to do the test with you. This could be a date, friend, family member, or anyone you choose.

3. Each take a copy of your word list. Each choose 5-10 words from the list to "show" to the other nonverbally.

4. Without saying anything, or letting the other person see your words, explain that you will take turns trying to communicate your feelings nonverbally. Sitting across from each other, assume a posture that you think shows feeling number one. Use posture, leg position, arms, hands, tilt of the head, brows, facial expression, eyes, etc. Hold a position for about 30 seconds to give time to write down their guesses.

5. Allow 3 guesses each time. If your partner is correct the first time, you get 10 points. If correct on the second guess, 7 pts., and if correct on the third guess, 3 points.

6. Now it's your partner's turn to "show" you a word. Continue this procedure until you have used up your words.

SCORING

The higher the score, the better. If you try the same "feeling" with several different people, it becomes clear whether or not the lack of clarity is in how you do it, or in how a particular person interprets. Consider this as you evaluate your nonverbal skills.

WORD LIST

Abandoned	Absentminded
Adoration	Affectionate
Aggressive	Assertive
Aloof	Angry
Annoyed	Anxious
Brave	Burdened
Calm	Capable
Caring	Challenged
Cheerful	Childish
Clever	Confused
Considerate	Curious
Crushed	Cynical
Deceitful	Defensive
Dependable	Degraded
Depressed	Desirous
Disappointed	Eager
Embarrassed	Emasculated
Enthusiastic	Envious
Exhausted	Fascinated
Fearful	Helpless
Horrible	Hurt
Impatient	Inadequate
Inept	Irritable
Joyous	Lazy
Left Out	Lonely
Loving	Miserable
Moody	Nervous
Offended	Playful
Powerful	Quarrelsome
Remorseful	Restless
Rejected	Shame
Saying, "no"	Sexy
Shocked	Silly
Sneaky	Stubborn
Suspicious	Tense
Timid	Turned On

Vindictive   Vulnerable
Wonderful   Worried
Worthless   Wounded

TO DO LIST

- Evaluate your own communication style, both verbal and nonverbal. Ask yourself if you are satisfied with it. Are you able to ask for what you want without apology? Express your feelings without accusation or defensiveness?
- Check the bibliography and read something on Assertive Training.
- Discuss styles of communication with a friend you trust to be honest, yet kind, and ask him/her to make suggestions as to how you can improve the way you come across.
- Depending on your responses, call the nearest college and inquire about classes or workshops in communication or Assertive Training.
- Add to the draft of your contract a specific way to enhance your communication or assertive skills.

1 Cera McFadden, First printed in New Choices, "Living Even Better After 50." March 1995.

Sexual Challenges

CHAPTER 7

CONFLICTING SEXUAL SIGNALS

Expectations are the most perilous form of dream, and when dreams do realize themselves it is in the waking world; the difference is subtle but often painfully felt.

Elizabeth Bowen, *The Death of the Heart*

Every culture has developed a set of mores and rituals to control sexual communication, childbirth, and in more developed countries, rights of inheritance. There is a universal recognition that without some checks and balances, the possibility of misuse of power, or exploitation, exists. Whether these controls take the form of chastity belts, or religious exhortations to "overcome the sins of the flesh," or laws against bigamy, societies deny free sexual expression in the interest of order in the arrangements of relationships between human beings. Different cultures dictate how much expression is allowed, from violent actions like who can kill whom, to lesser deeds like who can hug, and who can cry. "It is generally believed," according to feminist author Marilyn French, "that repression and regulation are necessary to control the two major sources of human disruption, aggression and sex."

HISTORICAL PERSPECTIVE

In *Your Perfect Right: A Guide to Assertive Living,*[1] author/psychologists Robert Alberti and Michael Emmons sum up what has been happening in this country during the past two decades. "There has been much emphasis on techniques of better sex. Kinsey may have started us off, but it was Masters and Johnson who guided us through the physical revolution stage. Now the media has proclaimed the 'sexual revolution' over. *Time* magazine devoted a 1984 cover story to the reduction of America's obsession with pure sex. We have moved from a time of heavy emphasis on the physical aspects of sex to a focus on the relationship aspects. Instead of exploring for new erogenous zones, we are talking about true intimacy, about devotion and commitment."

Alberti and Emmons go on to say that some see this as a swing back to the "good old days." "It seems more accurate," he writes, "to consider the entire process an evolution, of which the 'revolution' was a key part. The new emphasis on commitment incorporates the gains made through increased sexual expression. There is no return to old times, or forgetting about recent discoveries."

On the following page is a copy of a chart from *Your Perfect Right* showing former expectations and current expectations of females and males.

Unfortunately expectations, and even morals, are still unclear and confusing. Marilyn French posits that women and men, in general, have different moralities because they have different goals. She writes, "Male morals are designed to permit male transcendence... Female morals are designed to foster survival..."[2] In some cultures sex is not acceptable except when it becomes an instrument or expression of control; that is, when it is merely a part of power, and not a separate and unrelated element. French

FEMALE AND MALE SEXUAL ATTITUDES AND BEHAVIORS [1]

Females

Former Expectation	Current Expectation
Passivity	Equality
Misguided Compassion	No-nonsense Compassion
Silence and Suffering	Outspoken Enjoyment
Giving in	Initiation
Doing Your Duty	Active Participation
Hinting	Straightforwardness
Manipulation	Honesty
Shyness/ Embarrassment	Confidence, Playfulness
Fragility, Weakness	Strengh, Helpfulness

Males

Former Expectation	Current Expectation
Silence	Expression
Lack of Emotion	Openness, Flow
Insulation	Involvement
Strength	Vulnerability
Control	Mutuality
Machismo	Gentleness
Inflexibility	Patience
Exploitation	Equality
Score Keeping	Responsiveness

explains that there are some realistic grounds for men to feel they give up control to a woman in sex. Women can fake a pleasure they do not feel; their arousal is not visible. And women who are owned or rented frequently do fake pleasure, for excellent reasons. "Some women lie passively inert during sex, refusing to pretend a pleasure they do not feel. Some men feel desire for women they despise; this inevitably arouses repugnance after intercourse, and men's tendency is to avoid self-contempt by casting that repugnance on the woman alone." Partial gains can be misleading because progress is so uneven.

Differing concepts of power, and its role in sex, interfere with healthy sexual relationships. They result from a notion of sex as a controlling act, one of many expressions of domination, a function within a power relationship. To quote French again, "Mutual sex exists in a different dimension from sex as a form of domination; it exists in the realm of pleasure, to which power is irrelevant."

Underlying all efforts toward establishing mutual partnerships are the economic and political fabric of the society in which we live. Without economic equality, women still will be forced to remain in destructive relationships for economic survival of themselves and their children.

Contraception was probably the next most important milestone in sexual relations after the invention of the automobile (which provided the option of love-in-the-back-seat). Legalized abortion might be construed as another breakthrough, but tell that to someone who has been terrorized by Right-to-Lifers. Now we have AIDS. We seem to go two steps forward and one step back if you're an optimist, and one step forward and two steps back if you're a pessimist.

CONFLICTING INTERPRETATIONS OF SEXUAL SIGNALS

Sandra wears tight mid-rift tops with no bra, extremely tight jeans, and excessive make-up and jewelry. She flirts when she's out with Joe. He suffers in silence. One night a tough looking character grabbed Sandra and tried to kiss her. She screamed. Joe felt he had to fight the fellow even though he was scared. They got away, but he really let her have it for putting them both in that position.

Sandra protested that she thought he liked it when other men noticed her. He'd commented on how much attention she got from others and she thought he meant it made him proud.

It took a long time and much discussion for them to make their positions clear, and for them to work out compromises about what they both felt was reasonable in terms of dress and flirtatiousness. If Joe had been beaten up, it would have led to a different scenario. After this breakthrough, however, they were able to talk about their expectations in other aspects of their relationship. They began to express their feelings, which led to mutual understanding. After that they went on to making some long overdue ground rules about other issues such as the use of condoms.

CONFLICTING SIGNALS RE: ROLE EXPECTATIONS

Another example of conflicting expectations is Michelle's erroneous assumption that her husband wanted her to stay in a dependent role.

At forty Michelle let sixty one year old Abe, do all the driving, carry her suitcase, and do all the heavy lifting, feeling that any protests would make her seem "emasculating," less feminine, or bossy. Again, it took a crisis to get them to open up to each

109

other. After a heart problem was diagnosed Abe told her how resentful he was of her dependence on him and her taking his efforts for granted.

After many, "Why-didn't-you-tell-me's" they realized how much better it would be if they were both much more forthcoming in their communication. They then discussed their sexual needs instead of worrying in silence about the impact of his medication, and whether intercourse would be too stressful.

Confusing signals lead to jealous misunderstandings and resentments between partners if they are hidden from each other even if the secrecy is well-intentioned. When you believe that your partner's expectations of you are excessive, do something before your relationship is contaminated. If you deny your own needs and do whatever he/she asks of you, you may win the martyr-of-the-year award, but also suffer a sense of powerlessness, resentment, rage, decreased self-esteem, or all of these emotions.

Here is another example of the need to clarify expectations through direct communication:

Martha and Earl, both in their seventies, were haunted by the fear that Earl might have contracted AIDS as a result of a blood transfusion during a past illness. Martha approached his doctor behind Earl's back, then came home and told him the doctor said he needed an HIV test. He was deeply hurt that after forty some years of marriage she didn't approach him directly.

Ambiguous signals, especially in the sexual area, can lead to game playing that rarely accomplishes the goal of sparing a partner hurt. In fact, it often backfires and more hurt occurs than if clear signals were used in the first place.

If you have reservations about your partner's sexual behavior, health habits, or lack of communication, take the assertive route. If you feel your girlfriend or boyfriend is acting inappropriately, don't tackle the subject aggressively, don't make accusations, don't clam up, pout, threaten, or get hysterical. And do not go behind his/her back. Gently, but firmly, state how you feel. The challenge is to take responsibility for your feelings. Don't blame your partner for them. Don't say, "You **made** me feel..." or "You **make** me feel..." Say how **you** feel without blame.

You are an expert on your own feelings, so don't accept responses like, "you shouldn't feel like that," or "you don't really feel that way." Follow up your expression of feeling with a request or a statement about what you expect or hope for. Endless venting of feelings without any proposal of something your partner can do will leave him/her feeling angry or helpless or both. Listen well to your partner's feelings, hopes, and expectations.

When you both face the realities of your situation, and talk about them, you will feel as if a weight, like an anchor, has been lifted from you, and progress, whether apart or together, will be easier to envision.

DO MEN AND WOMEN COMMUNICATE DIFFERENTLY?

Men and women may have different expectations of themselves or each other because of their gender roles whether these roles are determined culturally or physiologically. The public is now being regaled with the notion that men and women have such different styles of communicating, such different needs in terms of self-expression, that it's difficult to get the twain to meet. Some new schools of thought regarding communication theorize that if men and women aren't connecting it's a "man thing." They suggest men are raised to express just two emotions in our society: anger and sex, and they don't know how to express anything else. They cannot say something like, "If you go to work full time I'll feel lonely and neglected," and ask for some reassurance. That would interfere with the self-image of a "he-man."

On the other hand, women, according to these theories, can only deal with their anxieties with talk; men want solutions, action, while women want relationship and conversation. The need to talk is supposed to be a "woman" thing that members of the male species are incapable of understanding. They can't "just listen," and women can't curb their need to talk.

This is not all nonsense. But the fact is that men and women are not from different planets, are all inhabitants of planet earth; there are women of action and male talkers. Understanding our differences is useful in forming close relationships in the context of which we can ask each other about health matters. "Have you been tested for AIDS?" "Are you interested in more than a one-night-stand?" If we emphasize sexual differences beyond the reality, we fall into stereotypical assumptions like, "He/she would never understand, so why bother to discuss it?" Or, "If I told her about my embarrassment she'd think I was a wimp." Or "If I tell him what I'd really like to do he'd think I'm a nymphomaniac. He'd be shocked."

Think of all the ways in which men and women are alike. They both want the same kind of loving relationships, ones that include trust, good communication, and mutually satisfying companionship. They also want loyalty that, like all the other qualities, can be discussed. If they can't talk about their feelings, differing expectations or assumptions can lead to hurt feelings. If such debacles do occur, if good communication has been established prior to the hurt, a resolution is much easier to attain.

MODERATING RELATIONSHIPS

But what do you do when you want to end an intimate relationship with someone you must continue to see regularly at work or in school, or in you neighborhood?

Suppose your ex-to-be is a decent person and you don't want hurt his/her feelings. You want both of you to feel comfortable when you see each other, yet you do not want more than a casual friendship.

If you have an opportunity, before the relationship goes too far, define the relationship you want in a positive way. For example, perhaps after a good dinner out, and expectations are not clear, you might say, "I'm so glad that we've had this evening. I feel that I know you so much better, and it will be more comfortable when I see you at work (or wherever). You will be more like a friend than a stranger." That might be enough to set the boundaries. If you do enjoy the person, you might even add, "Let's do this again in a month or two, so we can catch up on...(something you talked about)." This not only makes your position clear, but it also saves the other person the embarrassment of asking you out for the next week (or day) and being turned down. "Saving face" is extremely important in some cultures, and none of us like out-and-out rejection.

THE RIGHT TO SAY "NO"

In training for assertive communication and behavior, it is pointed out that unless you feel that you have the **right** to say "no," and to ask for what you want, you cannot refuse demands or communicate your needs effectively. How can a child bride, for example, say "no" to sexual intercourse when consent is not an issue, it's a "given;" where dowries are used as clubs and "marital rights" still supersede human rights?

In most Western cultures, however, the right of refusal does exist. If you signal a person that you are not interested in starting or continuing a relationship with him/her, and he/she persists with unwanted advances, it's time for you to affirm your right to say "no" and send strong deterrent signals.

THE TWO STEP "NO"

"There are many times in loving relationships," wrote Veronica Ray in *Meditations on Self-Esteem*, "when it's appropriate and necessary to say no...The times to say no are when we feel threatened, pressured, or coerced into doing something we don't really want to do; when we feel angry or resentful about doing something for others; and when examination of the request shows that harmful consequences for ourselves or someone else would be the result." If the other person has made it clear that they want you to do something that you don't want to do, or would like to continue a relationship you don't choose to, and you wish to stay on friendly terms, try the traditional two-step "no." First, validate the other person and acknowledge their right to ask. It's always acceptable to ask for anything as long as you leave room for the other person to say NO. Second, say NO. For example:

Step I: Validation

I feel complimented (or honored, or flattered) that you are interested in spending more time with me (and tonight has been fun — if it has).

Step II: The "No"

What I need right now, however, is to keep our relationship as a casual one. I respect you, and trust that you will understand.

Another example

Step I: Validation

Thank you for the invitation. It makes me feel good that you want to go to the concert with me (or spend more time together, or date) and I'm confident that you'll have no problem finding someone who will jump at the chance.

Step II: The "NO"

> Unfortunately, my interests are in a different direction right now. I would love to keep our relationship friendly as it is, without any other sense of commitment or obligation. I hope you're okay with that.

With this approach the person is apt to feel that his/her request is rejected, but not his/ herself as a person.

Whatever words you choose, be as clear, truthful, and kind as possible without using honesty as a weapon or an excuse to hurt the other person. Avoid phrases like:

- "I don't want to hurt your feelings, but..."
- "I hope you won't take this wrong, but...."
- "Please don't get angry when I tell you that..."

These are almost guaranteed ways of getting misunderstood, and of getting hurt, angry responses. Don't say what you don't want! What you say will stick, especially in an emotionally charged situation.

How much better it is to hear, "I trust you will understand when I tell you that..." or, "Thank you for being patient with me when I tell you that...." No guarantees, of course, but you certainly can change the odds! By suggesting a possible feeling or reaction, you increase the likelihood the person will choose that one. Far better, if someone is raging, to say, "You look mad enough to throw that pillow clear across the room," than "You look like you want to punch me!" By giving the person a positive way to deal with their feelings, you help "save face" again, and leave the door open for further, healthy dialogue.

ENDING RELATIONSHIPS

Lynne and Larry had a nasty divorce and when Larry exercised his visitation rights their fighting continued in front of the children. He pressed her for intercourse even though their divorce was final, and she allowed herself to be seduced once or twice compounding their ambivalence and confusion. Finally, with the help of a mediator, and focussing on what was best for the children, they came to some agreements about their behavior in front of the children, and what to expect of each other.

Clarifying their conflicting expectations earlier would have spared damage to the children's emotional health, and the expenditure of thousands of dollars in lawyers' fees.

Sharon and Bob had an intensely romantic relationship. Much loving sentiment was expressed. Bob repeated, "I'll always take care of you," and Sharon would often say, "All we need is each other." They didn't want anything mundane, humdrum, or tedious to mar their tender passion. The humdrum included contraceptive measures and discussion of practical matters.

When Sharon became pregnant she assumed that Bob's protestations, that he would always take care of her, included care of their baby. Bob assumed that "All we need is each other" precluded a third party, even, or especially, a child.

When romantic illusions get in the way of checking out each other's expectations realistically, tragedy can ensue. Different values in regard to abortion further polarized Bob's and Sharon's expectations. A sadder but wiser Sharon said her hopes, dreams, and romantic illusions "were wrecked, sunk to the bottom of the sea." Longer term relationships are more complicated, and may require a lot more discussion. It is important to talk if your partner is willing and able to do so. Sometimes good communication about parting changes an ending into a new beginning!

If the other person refuses to discuss the situation, you may resort to writing, or communicating through another person. The more effectively you communicate, the more apt you are to achieve mutually satisfactory closure. Also the more likely the other person is to follow the example, and the better you will feel about yourself and the ending.

The way you want to end a relationship is influenced by more than your own unique personality and preference. One influence is the length of time of the relationship. If it's a "one night stand," you say "never again." Long term marriages and long term relationships are at the other extreme. Another influence is the amount or degree of contact you want following the "ending." This varies from the termination where you want absolutely nothing to do with this person ever again to a situation where you want to end sexual intimacy but maintain friendly, daily contact, as when there are children involved, or you work in the same office.

Some people have great difficulty with endings. Avoidance and denial can be strong. Some even say, "I don't do endings." For example, there is the husband or wife who just doesn't come home; not even a note of goodbye. Or the person who makes a date or appointment and then doesn't show. Rather than face the other's reaction to ending, they split. More common is being together for a last time and pretending that it is business as usual. The fear and discomfort of endings keep some from entering relationships at all!

Other people have actually destroyed long term relationships because of something in their pasts they can't bear to talk about, like a one night stand. Denial and avoidance can work on some level to cause endings. But these kinds of endings seldom leave you with a sense of inner peace or high self-esteem. Seldom do they leave you with a strong, positive willingness to try again.

ENDING DANGEROUS RELATIONSHIPS

The importance of being clear, direct, and self-protective is illustrated in countless news stories of tragic endings of affairs and marriages. The number of murders perpetrated by ex-boyfriends, and ex-girlfriends, too, who refuse to be "exes" is staggering.

What do you do when the other person has different expectations of the relationship than you do? Or is more interested in pursuing it, whether it has been sexual or not? Unfortunately, in dangerous, potentially violent situations, escape in the night may be the only way. If you are caught in such a situation, get help, so that when your current relationship is ended, you can embark again on your pursuit of happiness.

TO DO LIST

1. Review the relationships you've had in the past. Have any of them been characterized by differences in role expectations?

2. Role-play different ways of saying "no," diplomatically, including the "two step NO."

3. Check out the expectations of behavior that your partner holds. Are they compatible with yours?

4. Check the communication section of your sexual self-contract. Is there anything you want to add? For example: how you will end a short term or longterm relationship?

[1] From YOUR PERFECT RIGHT: A Guide to Assertive Living (Seventh Edition) ©1995 by Robert E. Alberti and Michael L. Emmons. Reproduced for Eugenie G. Wheeler by permission of Impact Publishers, Inc., P.O. Box 1094, San Luis Obispo, CA 93406. Further reproduction prohibited.

[2] Reprinted with the permission of Simon & Schuster from BEYOND POWER by Marilyn French. Copyright © 1995 by Belles-Lettres, Inc.

CHAPTER 8

CONTROLLING EMOTIONAL CURRENTS

When anything is bothering you emotionally, healthy sex is probably one of the first things to be impacted. It is difficult to "get in the mood" when you are emotionally upset. It has a chilling effect on all aspects of your life. If you are in a relationship, your partner may feel rejected or blamed. If you are on your own, you are likely to seek out destructive sex or avoid all companionship. Several aspects of emotional well-being are particularly linked to intimacy, and deserve a close look.

ARE YOU DEPRESSED?

Depression comes in many forms. **Reactive depression** is the sadness that comes after a loss or disappointment. It is a reaction to something that happened to you in your life. Except in the acute phase, when the shock of a loss is new, this is the type of depression least likely to interfere with your loving.

When a partner shows caring and empathy, it can lead to more extended loving for comfort and/or distraction.

Your response depends on the severity of the loss, of course, and on your personal pattern of coping with loss. Generally the best plan is to talk about it with your friend or partner somewhere other than the bedroom. Then, when you want to be loving, it is easier to put the issue aside.

Endogenous depression is the name given to the kind that is caused by a chemical imbalance in your system. It is more long term, and usually requires medication, therapy, and careful attention to diet and exercise. This type of depression is characterized in part by a loss of interest in everything that was fun before the onset of the depression, including sex. Sometimes endogenous depression runs in families.

Another indication of endogenous depression is a disturbed sleep pattern, like waking up at two or three in the morning and not being able to get back to sleep. When you have this kind of depression much of your energy goes into fighting the depression. This leaves little energy for loving or nurturing a loving relationship. If you suspect this type of depression in yourself or your sexual partner, it is wise to consult your physician. It might save your marriage or relationship! The good news is, this depression is usually treatable. With professional help most people get it under control.

Another category is **seasonal depression.**

Jared and Colleen had been together for many years, and had two children together. They finally sought counseling one February. The winter months had always been hard, but they had attributed it to his work, which kept him happy and busy in the summer, but left him rather bored in the winter. He became grouchy and irritable. He looked for excuses to avoid sex. This year he had supplemental work that he enjoyed. The excuse was gone, but the problem remained.

After careful assessment it became clear that Jared was suffering from "seasonal" depression which is related to insufficient sunlight. Jared's treatment included full-spectrum lights. His and Colleen's relationship had been on the brink of disaster but soon became healthy and happy again.

The most important thing to remember about depression is to watch for it. If you suspect it, check it out. Acknowledge it. Then you are in a position to change it. It is much easier to treat the depression than to build a loving relationship around it. Depression makes a lousy bed partner.

ARE YOUR FEARS GETTING IN YOUR WAY?

Fear can be a great destroyer of intimacy. Anxiety is a common response to fears, and it can build until it is out of proportion to what started it. Uncomfortableness about new experiences is normal, and can lead to good communication and increased intimacy. However, when fear and anxiety interfere with intimacy, it is often because they are responses carried over from experiences or relationships from the past.

Cliff and Joanne met through a friend, and were immediately attracted to each other. After several months of a whirlwind relationship, they began to talk marriage. Cliff started talking about needing "space." Joanne was puzzled. The more she tried to please him and be available for him, the more he resisted. He said he loved her more than anyone, but wasn't ready for a commitment.

Cliff reluctantly agreed to counseling. In talking about his childhood, it became apparent that his mother, although she loved him, was not emotionally available to him. He would go to her with a hurt, and she would say, "be a big boy." He would be excited about a good grade, and she would say, "great," but never really pay attention.

He learned quickly that when someone says they love you it doesn't mean they will not let you down. It was so painful that rather than risk that kind of pain, Cliff mistakenly "decided" as a child (not necessarily consciously) not to let anyone be so important to him that they could hurt him like that again. Once he saw the dynamics of his emotional pattern, and grieved the pain of loss of his mother's support, he was able to commit to a relationship with Joanne that gradually grew in depth and trust.

Fears can also result in a lack of trust in yourself, because you made bad choices in the past. You don't trust your judgment in selecting a new partner. You fear you will repeat old, destructive patterns.

Fears need to be faced and talked about. Name your fear as clearly as you can, and then check it against reality. If someone else were to tell you a similar fear, would you find it logical? Find a way to work through your fears before you make major relationship decisions.

DO YOU HAVE COMPULSIONS THAT NEED TO BE ADDRESSED?

Melanie did not derive much satisfaction from her too-frequent sexual encounters. On the contrary, she didn't experience orgasm, and was always feeling empty rather than fulfilled. She saw her pattern as a quest and thought her constant hope for a better kind of relationship was normal and rational until some friends confronted her convincingly with not only the risks she was taking, but also how jaded she was becoming.

Compulsive sex is discussed in *You Can't Afford the Luxury of a Negative Thought:*

Some people seek sexual highs the same way drug and alcohol abusers seek chemical highs. Just because sex is "natural" (non-chemical) doesn't mean it can't be abused. It can. What you do sexually is not the issue. Why you do it is. Is it an expression of love for another, or is it a way of avoiding some inner feeling — loneliness, for example? Compulsive sex, like any lust, carries the following message: "I'm not enough as I am. I need something or someone out there to make me happy. Without that, I'm worthless."

Even with help from her friends, and sincere resolve on her part, Melanie was not able to stick to her new sexual policy. She then realized her problem was deep and she needed professional counseling. In this case, Melanie's inability to fulfill her own contract enabled her to face the reality of her situation and obtain the kind of help she needed.

If you are subject to compulsions or obsessive behaviors that are interfering with your building healthy sexual relationships, refer to your contract. Are you having difficulty in sticking to it? Take your inability to put it to use as a clue that you may need therapy. Think of this clue as a step in making your decision.

If you or your partner have problems such as alcohol or other substance abuse, an inclination toward sado-masochistic sexual practices, or other patterns that interfere with good sexual communication, trust, or enjoyment, seek psychiatric counseling for help in getting on track.

CAN YOU GET PAST SEXUAL ABUSE?

Fortunately, the answer is yes. Unfortunately, it may take a lot of work. A lot of support from a loving partner can certainly help. Child sexual abuse or rape can have an impact on a person's sense of themselves and his/her ability to trust in intimacy. If your first sexual experiences are associated with pain and fear, you need to acknowledge it and do the emotional work required to push past it. Even though the process may be difficult, the sense of relief and wholeness that results is worth the effort. Remember, it's a step away from toxic relationships and toward achieving the loving kind you want.

WHEN ARE YOU EMOTIONALLY HEALTHY?

Emotional Health does not mean you are free from mood swings, disappointments, and pain. What it does mean is that you have confidence in your ability to handle the emotional challenges that come your way. In a healthy relationship you and your partner can talk about emotional issues as they arise. You can both share feelings honestly, and take full responsibility for them. Blame is not an issue. Healing is the goal.

Instead of facing each other when you talk about heavy issues, sit side by side. Face the "problem." When you face each other it is easier to feel like antagonists, or like someone has to win or prove something. Instead, the person who feels the emotional pain can say what it is. This then becomes the issue or challenge that you work together to solve.

Sometimes the pain is so deep and complex that you need outside help. Don't bring parents, children, or friends into this process (or onto the healing team) unless both of you agree. Usually this builds resentments and makes it worse. You may have a mutual friend that loves you both and has good ideas. Or you might agree on consulting a counselor. As long as you both agree. Sometimes it is necessary for one person to reach out for professional help before the other one agrees to it, especially if you do not have good communication.

You will know when you and your partner are developing an emotionally healthy relationship because you will feel closer after a painful discussion instead of further apart. Working through emotional issues together is a bonding experience. Building your emotional health with a partner is a "win-win" situation.

124

TO DO LIST

- Take an inventory of your emotional reactions. For several days, several times a day, note on a scale of 1-10 whether your mood is high or low. Watch for a pattern. See what you can learn about yourself from this.

- Each day think of at least one thing to do that gives you positive emotional feelings. (If you can't do this, check out depression.)

- Choose an emotion (anger, fear, joy, sadness, pleasure) and write down as many things as you can that trigger that feeling. It will help you know your self better.

- Add to your sexual self-contract a plan for evaluating your emotional responses. Also, include a way to reinforce yourself.

Sexual Challenges

CHAPTER 9

NAVIGATING IN AN AGE OF SEXUALLY TRANSMITTED DISEASES

The most violent element in society is ignorance.
Emma Goldman in *Anarchism*

Staying healthy, avoiding sexually transmitted diseases including AIDS, is a major concern in charting a course to a loving relationship.

Bonnie was thrilled when Randy asked her for a date. Her roommate's response was that she should be thrilled. Randy dated a lot, both juniors and seniors. That hit Bonnie. Suppose with all that experience he'd contracted a disease, even AIDS? She decided to be careful. She was not in the habit of "jumping into bed" on a first date anyway, and was going to make sure it was safe physically before she took any chances.

Randy made her feel wonderful — he was suave, attentive, and full of praise for her. She decided it wasn't just sexual attraction. He discussed intellectual subjects and they loved all the same things. She knew she was so attracted that sex was inevitable. How to find out about his health status? She started with:

B: *You seem so sophisticated, I bet you've had a lot of experience.*

R: *Oh, I've been around a bit.*

B:. *Have you ever been in any trouble?*

R: *(Sounding hurt) What do you mean by that?*

B: *Well, I just wondered. There are so many risks out there these days.*

R: *What are you getting at?*

B: *Have you ever been tested for HIV?*

R: *Oh, so that's what's eating you. You don't have to worry. I'm clean. Look, you've already said I'm sophisticated, and you obviously are not. With the way we're getting to feel about each other, don't you think we should trust each other?*

Bonnie wanted to trust him. But should she?

AIDS

The AIDS virus (also called the human immunodeficiency virus or HIV) travels in the blood stream and affects the immune system. It prevents the body from effectively fighting infectious diseases so that HIV-infected persons can easily become ill with serious infections or cancers. When death occurs, it usually results from one of these diseases.

People with AIDS often appear healthy for a long time after becoming infected. Nearly ten years is the average length of time after a person becomes infected before disease symptoms begin to appear. AIDS is spread from person to person through the exchange of body fluids, such as semen and blood. For the most part, the virus is spread by sexual contact or by sharing drug needles and syringes with an infected person.

The costs of AIDS in human misery to the afflicted and their loved ones is incalculable. The economic costs are difficult to determine but estimates are that AIDS will siphon off an estimated total of eighty one billion to one hundred and seven billion dollars from the U.S. economy by the year 2000. Costs of the pandemic are already immense. The disease has run up a tab of seventy five billion dollars to date (1996), with three billion to six billion being spent on new infections each year. By the year 2000 the total cost to the global economy of the AIDS pandemic could reach five hundred and fourteen billion and, in the worst-case scenario, rob the world of 1.4% of its gross domestic product; the equivalent of wiping out the economy of Australia.

Despite costs and publicity about AIDS, sexually transmitted diseases are flourishing among the young. Like countless other young adults in the United States, Bonnie lacked skills for self-protection. How do you ask a partner if he/she has been tested for the AIDS or other sexually transmitted diseases? It's puzzling that this is happening when AIDS and safe sex are universal discussion topics for all ages. But the message is not getting through. One reason is embarrassment, and the fear that you'll be perceived as insulting, or lacking in trust or respect. Or you're afraid that you'll nip a potential relationship in the bud.

Even if you are educated and aware of the importance of using a condom for physical protection against life threatening disease, how do you insist on it in a romantic moment without antagonizing your partner? California's AIDS Education Campaign circulated a "wheel" of "Condom Comebacks" to help with what to say when your partner doesn't want to use a condom. The message was, "it doesn't matter how you say it, just find a way to use a condom with every partner every time. Protect yourself and the ones you love."

Following are some of the suggested rejoinders to pressure for sex without the use of a condom:

RESISTANCE TO USING A CONDOM	REJOINDER
It takes too long.	I love it when you take your time. What's the rush? I'll wait.
Just this once.	Only kids make decisions like that. It only takes once. No way.
It doesn't feel good.	AIDS feels worse. I'd feel better.
It spoils the mood.	It puts me in the mood. Not if I help.
You won't catch anything from me.	I forgot to take the pill. Condoms protect. Love doesn't. If you love me, respect my health.
Oh, come on!	No condom, no sex.

Ferd Eggan, an AIDS counseling coordinator, pointed out that safe sex campaigns were invented "during a period of time when people were hoping as hard as they could AIDS would be cured and that it they could just hold on with white knuckles everything would be O.K." But that is not the case. Safe sex is not a temporary prescription. It's for always and forever. "That's an extraordinarily difficult thing to ask of people," said Eggan. For some, the standard safe sex message is too absolute. "If the message is abstinence or death, use a condom every time, people who can't do that have no help at all." An alternative he suggests revolves around the concept of harm reduction: Use a condom, but if you can't always do that, at least do it for the riskiest behavior. Refrain from taking drugs and alcohol when you're having sex, but if you're not going to, plan ahead and make sure condoms will be in easy reach.

Set higher standards for yourself. The first step is to become informed about your needs, about sexual communication, and sexually transmitted diseases.

Only ignorance! Only ignorance! How can you talk about only ignorance! Don't you know that it is the worst thing in the world, next to wickedness? And which does the most mischief Heaven only knows.

Anna Sewell, *Black Beauty*

OTHER SEXUALLY TRANSMITTED DISEASES

Carrie thought she knew all about safe sex. She was cautious. When her friends began having sex in high school, she steadfastly refused. But, at 18, she fell in love and decided it was O.K. because this boyfriend seemed so nice, so safe. They didn't even discuss condoms.

Later, as the relationship faltered and Carrie learned more about her boyfriend's past, she decided to get tested for sexually transmitted diseases. After the exam, a clinic counselor told the tearful young woman that she had chlamydia, the most prevalent sexually transmitted disease in the country, which often produces no symptoms in women but can cause sterility if left untreated.

Shari Roan, Los Angeles Times

(October 26th, 1994)

Carrie, and countless other young adults, need to know that sexually transmitted diseases (STDs) are rampant and spreading. Health experts report that even in this age of AIDS, the naivete about the hazards of sex in the '90s is appalling, and means that countless people are at risk. STD infections boost the risk of contracting the human immunodeficiency virus, becoming infertile, or giving birth to babies with health problems.

Bonnie, mentioned earlier, was never able to convince Randy to be tested. He got tired of her nagging, so left her. But not until he had infected her with the HIV virus. A sad, but true story of a woman who didn't have the knowledge or skill to protect herself. Perhaps, with a self-contract and the skill and determination to put it into practice, her story would have had a better ending. At least now she's involved in trying to help other people avoid similar outcomes.

THE NEED FOR SEX EDUCATION

Health experts all recommend sex education in the area of STDs. Why is knowledge so important? It's relevant for young women but a background of information is necessary for all adults. Some of the reasons are:

- We are living in an increasingly promiscuous society in which people begin having unprotected sex younger and have more partners during their "unattached" period—often 10-20 years—before they commit to one monogamous relationship.

- Americans have an inability to talk about sexuality and provide factual sex education in the home, schools, and health care setting, even though the culture is highly sexualized.

- An antiquated approach to STDs by governments, health organizations and schools, makes it difficult for people to get treatment, screening, or even basic information.

Although HIV has helped raise awareness about all STDs, there is a common misperception that, other than HIV, the diseases are easily cured and cause no lasting harm. That is not true, according to Patricia Donovan of the Alan Guttmacher Institute. As infections permeate the population they lay a minefield of future reproductive problems, such as infertility, ectopic pregnancy and miscarriage. She explains that STDs often attack women silently, without symptoms.

This crucial bit of information rarely reaches young adults. For example, one 1990 study of college students in Canada found almost half didn't know STDs can be asymptomatic.

When you're entering or reentering the world of dating, at whatever age, a major concern should be your physical health. Denial of the risks is dangerous when an epidemic of sexually transmitted diseases exists. And an epidemic of STDs **does** exist — worldwide. Neglect of self-care often stems from a lack of awareness. Experts say that the biggest problem among both men and women may be that they don't perceive themselves at risk until it happens.

Gonorrhea and syphilis have been around for ages, and are still a problem. Several other sexually transmitted diseases have been identified only in the past two decades. The Alan Guttmacher Institute lists STDs as:

- **Chlamydia:** Bacterial. Often produces no symptoms in women. Men may experience discharge and burning sensation. Curable.
- **Genital Herpes:** Viral. Symptoms are often mild but can include aching or burning sensation and pain in legs or genital area. Blisters or painful sores may

appear and recur any time. Incurable, but a drug is available to reduce symptoms.

- **Gonorrhea:** Bacterial. Symptoms often absent but can include discharge, burning sensation and itching. Curable.

- **Hepatitis B:** Viral. No symptoms present in one-third of all cases but can cause fever, headache, muscle ache, vomiting and diarrhea. Infections often clear up by themselves, but some people become chronically infected. A vaccine is available to prevent infection.

- **HIV: Viral.** Often asymptomatic for many years. Later symptoms include immune system deterioration. Symptoms can be treated but infection is otherwise incurable to date (1996).

- **Human Papilloma Virus:** Viral. Produces painless fleshy warts. Warts can be removed but infection often reappears.

- **Syphilis:** Bacterial. Produces painless sores in early stages. Curable.

- **Trichomonlasis:** Parasitic infection. Women may have vaginal discharge and odor. Curable.

Sound sexual decision-making is based on realistic self-perception, awareness of consequences, and the power that knowledge provides.

AIDS AND THE MIDDLE-AGED

Hazel was commiserating with her friend, Janet who'd been widowed about a year. They were both in their early fifties:

Janet: *I appreciate your sympathy, but I've really gotten past the worst of it. Going out with Horace helps a lot. You know he's been a widower for fourteen years, so he really understands what I've gone through.*

Hazel: *I didn't realize you were involved. How long has this been going on?*

Janet: *Only a couple of months, but I've grown very fond of him.*

Hazel: *You'd better find out if he's been tested for AIDS.*

Janet: *How can you say such a thing? How can you even think such a thing? He's a fine, upstanding, older man and I wouldn't dream of vulgarizing our relationship by bringing up sex at this point.*

Hazel: *At this point?*

Janet: *Well, we haven't made love to that extent... And besides, he's so healthy. He's never had a blood transfusion or taken drugs so he's safe.*

Hazel: *But you know lovemaking is progressive. This man has been on his own for fourteen years. How do you know he hasn't been to a prostitute? How many affairs has he had?*

Janet: *Perhaps you mean well, but I find this discussion insulting and irrelevant.*

But Hazel had planted a seed. Janet forced herself to face the fact that she couldn't do what doctors can't do — she couldn't make a diagnoses regarding a serious disease based only on a combination of appearance (Horace's), and wishful thinking.

Janet, after much thought, realized that now, as a single person, more responsibility fell to her for herself and her decisions. First, she must learn about the risks that did not exist when she was dating her husband thirty years ago.

The next challenge was to integrate disease protection into her sexual negotiation with Horace. She hated the words "negotiation" and "power" applied to what she had with Horace. To her they were terms for the bargaining table in big business or union transactions. Broaching the subject of STDs delicately was difficult. Janet wasn't used to being so forthcoming. Remembering the contempt she had for her mother for playing coy games with her father, she realized she'd fallen into the same trap with Horace. She'd played on his sympathy a bit, acting weaker than she really felt because she assumed he enjoyed the role of the strong, protective male. If she stopped "playing dumb" would he still be attracted to her? Did she dare depend on her own strength instead of depending on or deferring to a man's?

It took courage but to Janet's surprise and relief, Horace was open to discussing the health issues, and appreciated her honesty. **He** had been afraid to ask **her** the cause of her husband's death for fear it had been AIDS. He hadn't wanted to offend her and was relieved when the whole subject was out on the table. He had more respect for her because of the courage she showed in bringing it out in the open. As a result their relationship reached a higher level of mutual honesty and closeness.

AIDS AND SENIORS

Older adults also need sex education. Some have contracted AIDS although it is far less common than in other groups. Misconceptions are that older adults are not at risk because if they have sex at all, it's in a monogamous relationship. But (according to the "Age Page" November, 1989, published by the National Institute on Aging) with increased age there tends to be a decline in immune system functions, making older people more susceptible to a variety of illnesses such as infections and cancers. Because of these changes in immune function, AIDS may affect older people differently than it does the young. Data from the Centers for Disease Control suggest that most older persons infected with the AIDS virus have developed disease symptoms more quickly than younger patients.

The older population also receives the highest rate of blood transfusions during routine medical care. As a result, the second most common cause of AIDS in people over age 60 (after homosexual and bisexual activity) has been exposure to contaminated blood transfusions received before 1985 when the public blood supply was not screened for the virus.

Paul Gann is a famous example. A political force in California, he died in September, 1989 at the age of seventy seven of pneumonia, a complication of AIDS, which was the result of a blood transfusion. Blood banks now offer the assurance of cleaner blood products. However, the number of older persons who received contaminated blood and who may now be unintentionally infecting spouses or other sexual partners remains unknown.

Medical experts predict that a cure or vaccine to prevent AIDS is not likely to be found in the near future. This means that responsibility for preventing the spread of AIDS rests on individuals. For example, making the choice to use condoms when sexually involved with someone other than a mutually faithful, uninfected partner, insisting on testing for the disease, and other decisions, are up to you. To make wise ones requires new knowledge, a must for every age group. We're in the middle of a serious epidemic. Shall we make it our business to learn more about what's going on in the world, or block our own learning by prejudicial assumptions?

So whatever your age, marital status, educational level, religion, or lifestyle, arm yourself with facts; with the empowerment that can come only from being informed. Stay involved in learning the skills that will keep you self-aware, assertive, and safe.

TO DO LIST

Take the following True/False test:

T   F

1___ ___ Older adults are not at risk of contracting AIDS because if they have sex at all, it's in a monogamous relationship.

2___ ___ Old people have little interest in sex.

3___ ___The greatest danger of rape is from a stranger.

4___ ___ AIDS is primarily a gay disease, so heterosexual people are not in a high risk category.

5___ ___ All's fair in love and war.

6___ ___ Except for HIV, and a few other very rare exceptions, sexually transmitted diseases are easily cured and cause no lasting harm.

7___ ___ Women are not at risk if they've only had sex with three or four men and never used drugs intravenously.

8___ ___ Today, one in five adult Americans carries some type of incurable viral infection such as herpes. When the curable bacterial Sexually Transmitted Diseases (STDs) such as syphilis and gonorrhea are included, Americans have at least a one-in-four lifetime chance of contracting an STD.

9___ ___ AIDS is the number one cause of death among Americans ages 25 to 44.

10__ ___Only 14 percent of sexually active unmarried heterosexuals who are not in monogamous relationships use condoms each and every time.

Answers:

1. False: According to "Age Page" Nov. 1989, published by the National Institute on Aging. With increased age there tends to be a decline in immune system functioning, making older people more susceptible to a variety of illnesses such as infections and cancers. Because of these changes in immune function, AIDS may affect older people differently than it does the young, but they are still susceptible.

2. False: If this is true, according to Hugh Downs in *Thirty Dirty Lies About Old* (G.K. Hall & Co., Boston, 1979), someone should have tipped off the likes of Strom Thurmond (United States senator from South Carolina), Leopold Stokowske, Charlie Chaplin, William O. Douglas — and who knows how many other lesser knowns — before they made the mistake of plunging into marriage in their older years with younger women. Three out of the four above produced children. And now the trend is for older women to go out with younger men. Elizabeth Taylor is just one example.

3. False: Most rapes are committed by someone the victim knows.

4. False: The misconception that AIDS is a "gay disease" may be one reason for the rapid spread of the epidemic.

5. False: War is never fair, and lack of fairness in "love" can result in life threatening disease, and death.

6. False: According to Patricia Donovan of the Alan Guttmacher Institute, that is not true. As infections spread through the younger population they lay the groundwork for future problems such as infertility, ectopic pregnancy and miscarriage. Sexually Transmitted Diseases attack women silently, without symptoms.

7. False: Female AIDS cases are on the rise partly because women can get infected more easily than men during sexual intercourse.

8. True: Studies done by the Center of Disease Control and Prevention report this to be true.

9. True: Also reported by the CDC.

10. True: Same Source. Incredible when you consider that we are in the midst of an epidemic.

* * * * *

Check your self-contract section "physical self-care." Have you included your decisions on how to protect yourself from AIDS and STDs?

CHAPTER 10

RED FLAGS AND STORM WARNINGS

*Of all pleasures, sex is the most intense... Freedom
is the state in which the greatest possible harmony
and sense of rightness obtains among body, emotions, and mind... To get to freedom of any sort, we
must get beyond gender roles and the definition of
man as the controller and woman as the controlled.*

Marilyn French

Beyond Power: On Women, Men, and Morals

Loving relationships cannot survive violence, the threat
of violence, or the fear of violence. Apprehension, or past
violent experiences can have a strong negative impact on
how you react in intimate situations.

In these times of increased fear, articles and TV programs about safety abound. Some give good advice on how
to protect yourself. However, by warning you of every
possibility, you can come away from a "safety" lesson
feeling more fear and more paranoia than before.

VIOLENCE AS A CULTURAL VALUE

Unfortunately it will take major cultural changes to stem the tide of violence in society. The media glorifies violence often making heroes of those who use it. Mike Tyson, a convicted rapist, is lionized. Television feeds us a steady diet of murder, sexual assault, and crime sending the message that violence is the way to resolve conflict. Our language reflects the constant linking of sex and violence: "He made a conquest," the emphasis on "performance" rather than connection. And the reverse, "She landed him." Accepting violence has become one of the values in our society, and that value must change if we are to be safe sexually and every other way.

If you are in a potentially explosive environment, plan a way to escape — to a friend's or neighbor's — or locate rape crisis centers in your area. Another good strategy is to join a support group. Get into therapy if you are not able to solve the problem on your own. In other words, if you sense such a threat, get smart, get help, or get out. This can be difficult. Age discrimination exists in this context along with sex discrimination. For example, one "safe house" wouldn't take an abused woman who was desperate because she was over 40 years old and didn't have any children. Programs to help men who are abused are almost non-existent.

THE USE OF POWER IN SEXUAL RELATIONSHIPS

As learned in the discussion of sexual goals, good sexual relationships are between two fellow human beings, not a powerful person lording it over a weak person. Differences can be fine, even enriching. Differences can complement each other. There can be value in diversity, but not if oppression or exploitation is involved. Henri Nouwen, a Catholic priest tells that caring is not an attitude of the strong toward the weak; caring takes place between equals. An effective approach to the prevention of violence is to strive for equality in sexual relationships. Equality in the workplace is a blow struck against sexual harassment of the weak by the powerful. Equal partnerships at home are not conducive to spousal abuse.

VERBAL AND EMOTIONAL ABUSE

It is important that you protect yourself from damaging sexual encounters. They may not hurt you physically, but can do serious damage to your sexual self-esteem. After you've raised your consciousness about what is being done to you, you need to strengthen your self-esteem to a point where you're less vulnerable to these tactics. Then you can learn to respond to them assertively. This skill is important because the wrong responses could inflame your tormentor and provoke violence.

Take an honest look at what, if anything, you do to provoke verbal abuse. If you are unnecessarily provocative, take corrective measures. If it is abuse by a partner, put any blame squarely where it belongs. Rid yourself of any self-blame, and refuse any guilt trips that anyone tries to lay on you.

How can you counter verbal abuse? One of the most effective de-escalators of verbal abuse is good listening. When frustrations mount, and are pent up inside, they can explode into violence. By helping someone to vent their fustrations, as opposed to taking them out on you, you are providing an outlet. It also helps to validate feelings. A supportive response is, "you have a right to feel that way." Everyone has a right to feel anyway they want to. We all have to take responsibility for our behavior, but our feelings are our own. Furthermore, they are not moral issues; they just are.

When empathetic listening and validation of feelings are not enough, more assertive responses are in order. Assertiveness is an extremely important skill because if your responses are aggressive, as opposed to assertive, they could make matters worse.

Brad is an example of a victim of verbal abuse:

Gloria verbally attacked Brad when he came home late. "Why are you late? Why can't you ever call me? You're so inconsiderate, insensitive, irresponsible, etc., etc.," followed by vicious name calling. He dreaded being the target for her tirades, stopped at a bar to fortify himself against them, and got home later and later.

Brad participated in an assertive training workshop where he learned that if he continued to stay away, or remained passive, the situation wouldn't improve. He was aware of the danger of aggressive counterattack, and felt he had no other choices. When it was pointed out to him that there were choices between the two extremes of passivity and aggressive behavior, he role-played assertive alternatives with enthusiasm. He practiced the "magic formula" for asking for what you want without blame:

When you_____ (an objective statement of the situation without accusation or blame. "When it" is even better if you can make it fit, as "You" sentences can come across as accusatory.)

I feel _____(You're taking responsibility for your feelings without blaming your partner, i.e. "You make me feel."

So would you please _____ (then your non-inflammatory request.)

The next time Gloria started an abusive tirade, instead of withdrawing passively for fear of coming on too strong, Brad said:

Gloria, when I'm yelled at_____

I feel attacked and want to stay away _____

So would you please talk with me quietly about this, and if we can't work it out, consider going with me to a marriage counselor?

Gloria was so surprised she was taken off guard and really listened to him for the first time in a long time. It's not unusual for a man to be subjected to verbal and emotional abuse by his wife.

Consider getting some training in assertiveness. Skillful communication can help you maximize what's positive in a relationship, but it also can help you protect yourself in a deteriorating one. If you've tried the above techniques and the verbal abuse escalates into violence, familiarize yourself with the resources in your community that provide help to victims. (See Resources listed in the Appendix.) It's empowering to know your rights so don't hesitate to seek legal advice, and in the meantime, check the "Victim's Bill of Rights" in this Chapter.

THE VULNERABILITIES OF MIDDLE-AGED AND OLDER WOMEN

Younger women are most at risk of being sexually assaulted. But a proliferation of articles, news stories, and autobiographies bear testimony to the vulnerability of the newly single women, whether widowed or divorced, in our current culture of confused sexual roles. Untold numbers of middle-aged women are walking targets for aggressive sex because of their lack of self-assertion, confusion about what they want out of life, predisposition to abuse drugs and alcohol, or tendency to look to others to meet their needs instead of looking to themselves.

The myth that older women are not sexually assaulted increases the vulnerability of one of the most vulnerable segments of the population. Assault is perpetrated by elderly husbands as well as by boyfriends both young and old. The fact that older women themselves buy into this myth further disempowers them. As a result they may take

145

unnecessary risks, may not take necessary precautions, or learn appropriate self-care strategies.

STEPS TO PREVENT/STOP VERBAL ABUSE:

The first step is awareness with objectivity. It's important that you know what's being done to you.

The second step is to take an honest look at what, if anything, you do to provoke verbal abuse, and to put any blame squarely where it belongs.

Step three is to build your self-esteem as best you can so that you will be less vulnerable to verbal abuse.

The fourth step is to get training in assertiveness. Skillful communication can maximize what's positive in a relationship, and also help you to protect yourself.

A fifth step is to familiarize yourself with the resources in your community that provide help to abused women, and use them appropriately.

A sixth step, if necessary, is to learn your rights.

CRIME VICTIMS BILL OF RIGHTS:

If you've worked hard at the above steps and find that reasonable communication cannot be sustained; if violence does occur, avail yourself of help. After crimes of sexual assault the trauma can be compounded by what the victim is forced to go through afterwards. Unfortunately, the aftermath can be dangerous because of the possibility of retaliation for fighting back or reporting the crime. It can feel dehumanizing when the victim is ignored by the justice system. Sometimes victims must wait in the same waiting room with the assailant. Often victims are not notified of the assailant's release into a nearby community posing a threat.

The Victims' Rights and Restitution Act of 1990 signed by Dick Thornburgh, Attorney General, states that a crime victim has the following rights:

(1.) The right to be treated with fairness and with respect for the victim's dignity and privacy.

(2.) The right to be reasonably protected from the accused offender.

(3.) The right to be notified of court proceedings.

(4.) The right to be present at all public court proceedings related to the offense, unless the court determines that testimony by the victim would be materially affected if the victim heard other testimony at trial.

(5.) The right to confer with the attorney for the Government in the case.

(6.) The right to restitution.

(7.) The right to information about the conviction, sentencing, imprisonment, and release of the offender.

Verbal, physical, and emotional abuse are serious deterrents to loving relationships whether between husband and wives or other partners. Prevention is the key, but when it does occur, you must take action whether that action is to become more assertive, to get counseling, escape, or see a lawyer.

TO DO LIST

1. Practice some of the de-escalating procedures in this chapter to be ready in the event that you are subjected to verbal abuse.

2. Become familiar with the agencies and resources in your community that serve people who are victims of sexual abuse.

3. Check to be sure you've included in your self-contract your choices about how you will deal with verbal, emotional or physical abuse.

4. Write into your sexual self-contract the name of the person(s) or agency(ies) that you will contact if you are ever sexually assaulted to assure you the maximum help and loving support.

CHAPTER 11

REPAIR THE DAMAGE

It is not the load that wears us down, but how we carry it.

Victor Frankl

If you have been a victim of a sexual crime of violence, you are not alone. Campus violence has grown alarmingly in the last decade. Half of all women murdered in the United States annually are killed by a current or former husband or boyfriend. If a relationship has gone on the rocks, and you feel hurt, what can you do to repair the personal damage? What can you learn from the experience that will help you start a new and better relationship in the future?

Sexual health, as defined by the World Health Organization in 1975, is the integration of the somatic, emotional, intellectual, and social aspects of sexual being, in ways that are positively enriching and that enhance personality, communication, and love. So how do you get there from here, when "here" is a climate of fear of pregnancy, AIDS, changing values, and mixed sexual signals? At any age it is difficult.

With an injury from sexual assault there is a need for healing. Emotional wounds last much longer and interfere with the victim's positive sense of her/his self as a sexual being and an intimate partner. There is no one right way to heal. Each person has her/his own best way. For some, it is years of intense therapy. For others it's a spiritual ritual, or through the support of a special friend, — or all of the above. How do you discover or create the best way for yourself?

THE BASIC AAA'S

Some basic truths apply to most situations requiring sexual healing. Let's start with the three A's: awareness, acceptance, and actualization.

AWARENESS

When you don't know when you have been spit on, it does not matter too much what else you think you know.

>   Ruth Shays in John Langston Gwaltney,

>   Drylongs (1980)

Before you can consciously work to change something you need to be **aware** of it. A man may ejaculate prematurely, but figure it's better than not at all. A woman may decide she didn't orgasm because she was too tired, or isn't built right. Or she may decide it isn't important. Whatever your negative sexual experiences, you could "write them off" or "shine them on" with excuses or blame. You could simply lower your expectations, or change your definition of who you are sexually to "frigid," "inadequate," "not interested," or "still waiting for Mr. Right," (or "the right girl,"). You may not even know that you need healing and are capable of it. Some, even after being raped, blame their own behavior, even though they were strong and clear with their "NO." They say, "After all, I was drinking," or, "Maybe because I was flirting I inadvertently asked for it," or "I shouldn't have gone with that person, or group, to this or that place." Sometimes they think, "He has a right, he's my husband." Studies affirm that marital rape is one of the most common forms of rape. (Groth, Nichols, and Birnbaum, Jean, *Men Who Rape: The Psychology of the Offender*, p 179, Plenum, 1979)

It's hard to heal the impact an experience has on your self-esteem if you perceive that experience as your fault. It's difficult to restore your sense of sexual self if you deny the reality of the traumatic effect it had on you. Being **aware** of the sexual experiences you've been subjected to, and that you've been injured, is an important first step.

The second step is to **accept** the reality, that it happened, and is a part of your history. Many victims waste hours and waves of emotion with, "If only...!" "If only I hadn't gone in to use the phone...," "If only I hadn't had that last drink...," "If only I had walked a different path...," "If only she had come with us...," "If only I had listened to...," "If only I had followed my instincts...."

To "accept" is to acknowledge to yourself that your experience was real. Wishing it could be different only drains you of your power to change how you respond to past events. Getting stuck on guilt distracts you. Further self-blame weakens you. Only with your acceptance of your personal reality are you ready to take the next step.

Even if you're on the right track, you'll get run over if you just sit there.

Will Rogers

To **actualize**, or take action, becomes easier as you grow in awareness and acceptance. You then have a basis on which to decide what actions you want to take that will give conscious direction to the choices you make. You want to make choices that minimize the likelihood of further harm, and increase the likelihood that you will get what you want. Taking charge of your present and future makes it easier to heal the past.

HEALING THE LOSS

Whenever there is injury, there is loss. For you it may be loss of power, esteem, or ability. It might be the loss of a feeling of trust and safety. Let's look at what is known about loss:

- Loss is a part of the natural cycle of all life.
- Some loss is involved in every change.
- One loss may trigger fear of other losses.
- All losses are not bad or undesirable.
- Even painful loss can be a great resource for learning.
- The gain may outweigh the loss.
- Loss of control can lead to loss of self-esteem.
- Feelings of guilt are natural.
- There is no "one right way" to deal with loss.
- The pain will get lighter.
- We can heal from loss.

In the field of bereavement several exercises have been devised to facilitate the grieving process. They're called "grief work" and can help you through some of the stages of grief such as denial, rage, depression, and finally to acceptance and moving on. If, as you've sought a loving relationship, you've been physically or emotionally injured and suffered losses as a result, some of the following exercises might help. Practicing whichever ones appeal to you can be healing, distract you from obsessing about your experience destructively, and help you to feel more in control.

EXERCISE I. ACKNOWLEDGING YOUR LOSSES

Think about a negative sexual experience, or a significant rejection. Whatever experience comes to mind first is probably the best one to start working on. Don't waste time deciding which was the worst, or where to start. With your experience in mind, think of it in relationship to each of the above statements about loss. How does it fit in this case? What thoughts or feelings are triggered? Take as much time as you need. Write notes to yourself if that will help.

As you acknowledge your loss or losses, you will likely bring forward your feelings of grief. In coping with grief, bear the following in mind:

- Grief is a natural, normal, healthy response to loss.
- Grief is a healing process that can be trusted.
- There is no "one right way" to grieve.
- How we grieve a loss is individualistic.
- Grieving a loss helps restore balance.
- Talking helps.
- Grieving can feel all consuming, but it isn't.
- Grief is something we move through to heal.

Once you accept your right and need to grieve, how do you "get on with it," so that the healing expands and the pain diminishes? Some people find physical ways to vent their anger. Others write letters to the person that harmed them, and then tear them up. Talking to a friend, support group, or counselor can be healing. Writing is also a good emotional outlet. Keeping a journal with emphasis on recording your feelings helps.

Experiment with those approaches and the following exercises until you find the healing strategy that works best for you.

EXERCISE II. FOCUS

A technique found to be helpful with veterans and others suffering from post traumatic stress disorder is to take a painful experience and write it out in as complete detail as possible. Write about the environment, the smells, the temperature, the sounds, the feelings. Allow and accept the feelings as you write. Acknowledge them, and let them pass.

When you're finished, read it and make additions or changes as more memories surface. Once you are satisfied that what you have written is a clear statement of what you experienced, find a person you trust and read it to that person. Explain to that person that you are not asking for advice or help. All that you want is for that person to listen with attention and caring. Read your focused story to as many people as you need to until it begins to lose some of its negative power for you.

EXERCISE III. IMAGERY

In a relaxed state, use your imagination and redo the experience the way you wish it had been. Be as detailed as possible. Begin a little before the incident, so you can choose to go somewhere else, or with a different person. Include sounds, smells, colors, shapes, feelings, thoughts. Let yourself live the good emotions you feel when something goes just as you want it to. Reclaim the good feelings. They belong to you. Choose to build positive feelings to overpower the negative feelings that you have taken on in relation to your experience. You can reprogram, as it were, the responses to the stimuli that are a part of your experience.

EXERCISE IV. AFFIRMATIONS

Affirmations are another approach to mastering your emotions and refocusing your thinking in a positive direction. They are clear, simple statements that affirm you and what you want. As you design your affirmations, be sure to get rid of anything negative. State what you want, not what you don't want.

Avoid sentences like "I won't let this ruin my life," or "I won't drink any more. . ." Affirmations work on your subconscious and at this level what is transmitted is the key words, so your unconscious would hear "ruin my life..." or, "drink more..."

Although affirmations need to be individualized to best meet exactly what you want, examples of positive ones are:

- I accept my personal history and value the person I am.
- I am strong and capable.
- I am in charge of how I respond to others.
- I've developed a sound self-contract and stick to it.
- I make choices that are good for me.

FORGIVENESS

According to Janice Harris Lord, author and Director of Victim Services for Mothers Against Drunk Drivers, "You will need to decide, based on your own life experiences and religious convictions, what to do about forgiveness. It is a difficult task. If others imply that you should offer forgiveness, tell them it is an important matter and that you will handle it in a manner that your integrity allows." She suggests that veterans of faith in most religions find something of an "abiding presence" in the midst of their suffering. They experience their God or Higher Being not so much as a solution to their problem of grief, but as a Companion who stands with them in the midst of it, and that gives them strength.

Lewis B. Smedes in *Forgive & Forget: Healing the Hurts We Don't Deserve* contends that we forgive in four stages. The first stage is **hurt**, "when somebody causes you pain so deep and unfair that you cannot forget it, you are pushed into the first stage of the crisis of forgiving." The second stage is **hate**, followed by **healing**. The fourth stage can be a **coming together** which obviously depends on the other person as well as you. Smedes recognizes that sometimes you have to heal alone.

Another concept of forgiveness is that "for giving" is giving the problem back to the person it belongs to. If someone has hurt you, and that person's behavior was negative, then that is that person's problem. You need to work on how you responded to the situation. It is not your job to make the other person feel sorry, or to make the other person wrong, or even aware. Your job is to give back to that person what is in their power, so you can reclaim your power to change the impact it had on your life.

Forgiveness is an individual decision. It can be very freeing if you achieve it. But if you feel that it would not be appropriate in your situation, that choice is yours.

TO DO LIST

In Linda Braswell's guide for survivors of rape and sexual abuse, *Quest For Respect*, she recommends some excellent "Steps You Can Take" in relation to safety and healing. For Example:

- Make a list of those people:

    Who you can tell.

    Who need to know.

    Who you want to know.

- Make a list of your fears. After each fear, write down how you are going to handle it.

- List your reasons for and against reporting/bringing charges against the person who harmed you.

- Identify the changes that have taken place in your lifestyle as a result of the assault.

- Assess what further changes you would like to make for more home security or to broaden your network or support system.

Use any of the above that you feel would be helpful to you. Incorporate them into your sexual self-contract if appropriate.

Sexual Challenges

CHAPTER 12

THE SAFE HARBOR OF A LOVING RELATIONSHIP

...our sexuality is a final frontier of privacy and autonomy any woman or man has the right, and need, to defend, according to personal values, in this invasive mass society where so little is left that we can control in our lives.

Betty Friedan, *The Second Stage*

A happy marriage, a loving long term relationship, are goals worth striving for. Your personal, sexual contract is a tool that facilitates your process toward your goal.

Now you are more aware of the importance of self-knowledge; that knowing yourself is an essential step toward positive change. You have examined obstacles such as sexually transmitted diseases, lack of insight or self-delusion, myths, mixed messages, differing expectations from a partner, depression, and violence. These are the hurdles that could block your route to your loving relationship. But you have faced them and made decisions about how you will confront and overcome these hurdles.

Now is the time to review your draft sexual contract, make any revisions that you wish, and complete it. This is the culmination of your work on it. Now you are ready to keep it an updated, viable, support as you progress toward your goal of a loving relationship.

REVISING YOUR PERSONAL SEXUAL POLICY

The desire to change your contract is apt to arise when certain dynamics happen. An understanding of these dynamics can be helpful as you make progress toward loving relationships. Insight about these conditions also increases your sense of personal power and control over your sexual experiences.

Sometimes you may want to change your contract simply because you didn't think through some aspect of it carefully enough. Whatever the reason, there's much insight to be gained from re-examining your policy. It's a challenging step in the process of claiming your sexual self.

Internal conflict about your self-contract may arise when old, negative patterns re-surface. When you are in a sexually charged situation, even though you are strong enough to stick to your policy, you may wish to change it. When you are alone again in a quiet, safe place, re-examine it. This creates an opportunity for you to challenge your behavior pattern and to change, or heal, the self-defeating ways, rather than change your carefully thought out contract.

Another occasion when you may want to revise your policy is when you realize that you are stronger than before and see yourself in a new light. You may have set a policy that did not really reflect the new, emerging person that you are becoming. If this happens you may see that some negative patterns were at work when you last set your policy. It can be exciting to validate your growth and determine a new plan.

The guidelines for changing your sexual self-contract are similar to the guidelines for writing the original. Review your existing sexual self-contract remembering what led you to your previous decisions. How were you feeling about yourself then as compared to now? When did you feel the strongest and healthiest?

The next steps toward sound revision are:

- Write down the change or changes you are considering adopting.

  This is your chance to explore all possible options again, just as you did in the beginning. If it helps, recreate in your mind the situation that led you to consider making a change. Be specific.

- Compare your old agreement or plan with the changes you are considering.

  Think about the possible consequences of any change. Role play specific hypothetical situations in your mind.

- Put your "new" (changed or reaffirmed) agreement with yourself aside. If feasible, wait a day, and then see if it still feels right to you. If so, use it. If not, repeat the process until you are satisfied.

COMPLETE YOUR CONTRACT

Congratulate yourself on taking an honest look at who you are and what you want. Reward yourself for any and all efforts you have made to understand and change patterns that have harmed you in the past.

Your contract will be your main support in your newly developed policy for reaching your goal.

BALANCE

Now you can bring a new degree of balance in your life. Balance is a key ingredient in loving relationships: balance between intimacy and wholeness, giving and tak-

161

ing, growing and resting. It's balancing yourself and your personal needs, and balancing your needs with those of your partner.

Balance means being able to negotiate differences so when your relationship does get off track, it is only for brief periods. In balanced relationships there is equality of power and each person is encouraged to reach his/here fullest positive potential with the loving support of a non-threatened partner.

USE YOUR CONTRACT FOR SUPPORT

Creating a loving relationship is like producing a work of art. Sometimes you feel inspired and it goes smoothly. Sometimes there are frustrations.

You will climb some mountains together, and support each other in your individual efforts. Each will glow with the other's successes, as well as provide comfort in the darker valleys. Your contract can be a source of support, and a steadying influence during difficult times. Make maximum use of it.

INGREDIENTS OF A LOVING RELATIONSHIP

Teamwork Concept

One ingredient of a loving relationship is teamwork. Michael Castleman, who has counseled hundreds of men with sexual problems, states:

> *Lovemaking is often compared to sports in the men's magazines through the use of phrases like "bedroom olympics." The metaphor is useful if we consider lovemaking as a team sport, with men and women on the same team. Good teamwork depends on the members understanding of one another's strengths and weaknesses, preferences and idiosyncracies. Team members should complement one another, not compete or take advantage of each other. The same goes for lovemaking.*

The Safe Harbor of a Loving Relationship

The safe harbor of a loving relationship is characterized by loyalty and trust, equality, fairness, compatibility, mutual goals, and enduring companionship. You and your partner can communicate on all levels: verbal, affectional, and sexual. The skills you've acquired in the process of developing your contract will help you provide these components of a communicative, nurturing, mutually supportive, relationship. In such a relationship each partner feels as concerned for the other's welfare as his/her own, loved and loving, and fulfilled.

In the safe harbor of a healthy, loving relationship you will have met your sexual challenges and will experience a peaceful sense of wholeness, belonging, and joy.

Bon Voyage.

BIBLIOGRAPHY

ARTICLES

Berstein, William C., M.D. *Sexual Dysfunction Following Radical Surgery for Cancer of Rectum and Sigmoid Colon*, "Medical Aspects of Human Sexuality" March, 1972

Hanson, Richard W., Ph.D., & Franklin, Michael R., Ph.D., *Sexual Loss in Relation to Other Functional Losses for Spinal Cord Injured Males*, "Archives of Physical Medicine and Rehabilitation," Vol.57, June, 1976)

Jones, Shirley, and Ingels, Marty, Front Line: She Said, He Said (page 30), "MODERN MATURITY", November-December, 1995

Kaplan, Stephen G. and Wheeler, Eugenie G., *Survival Skills for Working With Potentially Violent Clients*, "SOCIAL CASEWORK: The Journal of Contemporary Social Work", June, 1983, Family Service Association of America

Mantell, Joanne E., M.S.S.W., *Reducing Post-Mastectomy Sexual Dysfunction: An Appropriate Role for Social Work*, Paper presented at the 1977 National Association of Social Workers Professional Symposium, San Diego, CA

McFadden, Cyra, *Singles Dating: Happiness in the Minefield* "NEW CHOICES: For Retirement Living", March/April, 1995

Walker, Lou Ann, *Dangerous Liaisons*, "NEW WOMEN", September, 1995

BOOKS

Alberti, Robert E. & Emmons, Michael L, *Your Perfect Right: A Guide to Assertive Living.*, Impact Publishers, San Luis Obispo, CA 93406 5th edition, 1986

Braswell, Linda, *Quest For Resect: A Healing Guide for Survivors of Rape*. Pathfinder Publishing, Ventura, CA 1989

Castleman, Michael. *Sexual Solutions: An Information Guide.* Simon & Shuster, New York, NY 10020 1980

French, Marilyn, *Beyond Power: On Women, Men, and Morals*, Summit Books, NY, 1985

Friedan, Betty, *The Second Stage*, Summit Books, New York, 1981

Groth, Nichols, and Birnbaum, Jean, *Men Who Rape: The Psychology of the Offender*, Plenum Press, 1979

Hendrix, Harville, *Keeping the Love You Find: A Guide for Singles*

Jampolsky, Gerald G., & Cirincione, Diane V., *Change Your Mind, Change Your Life*, Bantam Books, New York, 10103, 1983

John Roger & McWilliams, Peter, *You Can't Afford The Luxury Of A Negative Thought: A Book for People with Any Life-Threatening Illness-Including Life*, Prelude Press, Los Angeles CA 90046, 1991

Lerner, Harriet Goldhor, *The Dance Of Anger: A Woman's Guide to Courageous Acts of Change in Key Relationships*, Harper & Rowe, New York, NY, 1989

Lord, Janice Harris, *No Time For Goodbyes: Coping with Sorrow, Anger and Injustice After a Tragic Death*, Pathfinder Publishing, Ventura, CA, 93003, 1987

Maggio, Rosalie (Compiled by), *Quotations By Women*, Beacon Press, Boston, MA 02108 1992

Parrot, Andrea; Cummings, Nina and Marchell, Timothy, *Rape 101: Sexual Assault Prevention For College Athletes*, Learning Publications, Holmes Beach, FL 34218-1338

Smedes, Lewis B., *Forgive & Forget: Healing the Hurts We Don't Deserve*, Harper & Row, San Francisco. CA 1984

Steinem, Gloria, *Revolution From Within: A Book of Self-Esteem*, Little, Brown & Co., Boston, MA 1992

Wheeler, Eugenie G., & Dace-Lombard, Joyce, *Living Creatively With Chronic Illness: Developing Skills for Transcending the Loss, Pain and Frustration*, Pathfinder Publishing, Ventura, CA 93003, 1989

Woititz, Janet G., *Healing Your Sexual Self*, Health Communications, Inc., Deerfield Beach, FL 33442, 1989

PAMPHLETS

Dickman, Irving R., *Sex Education for Disabled Persons*, **Public Affairs Committee, Pamphlet No. 531 1975**

Gambrell, Ed, *Sex and the Male Ostomate,* United Ostomy Association, Inc., 1111 Wilshire Boulevard, Los Angeles, CA 90017

ORGANIZATIONS

Athletes for Sexual Responsibility, University of Maine, Room 15, Merrill Hall, Orono, Maine 04469-5749

Men Stopping Rape, Inc., Box 316 306 N. Brooks St., Madison, WI 53715

The organization began in Madison, WI in 1983. It is one of the nation's largest and most active groups of men working to end male violence against women and against men. MSR has presented over 2500 workshops, the majority with male-only groups in high schools, fraternities, prisons and athletic teams.

National AIDS Hotline, 1-800-342-AIDS, 1-800-344-AIDS for Spanish, 1-800-AIDS-889 for hearing impaired

National AIDS Information Clearing House, P.O. Box 6003, Rockville, MD 20850

United Ostomy Association, Inc., 1111 Wilshire Boulevard, Los Angeles, CA 90017

VIDEOS

Gentleness Is Strength: Men Stopping Rape Documentary

Featuring footage of workshops, discussions and the 1990 rally and march for a world without rape. Produced by:

Men Stopping Rape, Inc.

Box 316 306 N. Brooks St.

Madison, WI 53715

Rape Awareness (26 minutes)

Using athletes as actors, this video portrays a series of three vignettes on "The Date" which ends in date rape, "The Morning After" about a party gang rape, and "Talking with Friends" where discussion implies it is the victims fault. These are discussed with suggestions for change to lead to a positive ending.

Available from **Athletes for Sexual Responsibility** ($80.00)

SMART SEX (20 minutes)

This is a second video by **Athletes for Sexual Responsibility.** With the rise in HIV infection, honesty may be the only policy. **Smart Sex** starts with getting in touch with all the messages...baggage... you have received about sex, how deeply you would like to be involved, and what your needs are. It means having the freedom to choose, and taking responsibility for your choices. ($80.00)

INDEX

ORDER FORM

Pathfinder Publishing of California
458 Dorothy Ave.
Ventura, CA 93003-1723
Telephone (805) 642-9278   FAX (805) 650-3656

Please send me the following books from Pathfinder Publishing:
_____ Copies of **Beyond Sympathy** @ $11.95 $____
_____ Copies of **Injury** @ $9.95 $____
_____ Copies of **Living Creatively**
                With Chronic Illness @ $11.95 $____
_____ Copies of **Managing Your Health Care** @ $9.95 $____
_____ Copies of **No Time For Goodbyes** @ $11.95 $____
_____ Copies of **Quest For Respect** @ $9.95 $____
_____ Copies of **Sexual Challenges** @ $11.95 $____
_____ Copies of **Surviving an Auto Accident** @ $9.95 $____
_____ Copies of **Violence in our Schools, Hospitals and**
                Public Places   @ $22.95 Hard Cover $____
                                     @ $14.95 Soft Cover $____
_____ Copies of **Violence in the Workplace** @ $22.95 Hard $____
                Violence in the Workplace @ $14.95 Soft $____
_____ Copies of **When There Are No Words** @ $9.95 $____
                                              Sub-Total $____
                Californians: Please add 7.25% tax. $____
                Shipping* $____
                                              Grand Total $____

I understand that I may return the book for a full refund if not satisfied.
Name:_____

Address:_____
_____ZIP:_____

*SHIPPING CHARGES U.S.
Books: Enclose $3.25 for the first book and .50c for each **additional**
book. UPS: Truck; $4.50 for first item, .50c for each additional. UPS
2nd Day Air: $10.75 for first item, $1.00 for each additional item.
Master and Visa Credit Cards orders are acceptable.